A Jewish Odyssey

One Woman's Life in America, Israel, and India

Saralea Zohar Aaron

Order this book online at www.trafford.com
or email orders@trafford.com

Most Trafford titles are also available at major online book retailers.

Note for Librarians: A cataloguing record for this book is available from Library
and Archives Canada at www.collectionscanada.ca/amicus/index-e.html

Printed in Victoria, BC, Canada.

ISBN: 978-1-4251-8700-2 (Soft)

*Our mission is to efficiently provide the world's finest, most comprehensive
book publishing service, enabling every author to experience success.
To find out how to publish your book, your way, and have it available
worldwide, visit us online at www.trafford.com*

Trafford rev. 10/16/2009

 Trafford PUBLISHING® www.trafford.com

North America & international
toll-free: 1 888 232 4444 (USA & Canada)
phone: 250 383 6864 • fax: 812 355 4082

DEDICATION

This book is dedicated
to the memory of my cousin Tsvi Weil and his family,
who were murdered by the Nazis at Auschwitz;
to Eli Cohen, Ada and Enzo Sereni, Jan Karski, Dr. Janus Korczak,
and the many others who risked their lives
so that the State of Israel might live;
and to every fellow Jew
with whom I sweated it out during the Yom Kippur War—
especially those who were permanently maimed or did not return.

Contents

ACKNOWLEDGMENTS

I COULD NOT HAVE WRITTEN THIS BOOK WITHOUT THE INSPIRATION AND HELP GIVEN ME BY MY FRIEND OF MANY YEARS, RABBI THEODORE SCHNEIDER. Equally indispensable has been the loyal support of my daughter, Dalya. She has kept up my spirits and been a very good critic. I am deeply grateful, as well, to Nan White of Cambridge Writers & Editors for her encouragement throughout this project, to the research librarians at the Boston Public Library, and to friends who typed the manuscript. In spite of all this assistance, I am sure my book has many flaws—errors of fact, documentation, or omission—for which I accept full responsibility.

I will be eternally grateful for the gifts from family members who are no longer living: the love of humanity I learned from my stepfather, Gerald Siegel, and from my "honorary uncle" and dear family friend, Ralph Hensey; the self-sacrifice and love of Judaism given me by my uncle, Joseph Swiatez, and by my maternal grandmother, Mama Tzipah. May their noble souls rest in peace.

FOREWORD

THIS BOOK MIGHT NEVER HAVE BEEN WRITTEN IF I HAD NOT FINALLY SUCCUMBED TO MANY YEARS OF ENTREATIES BY FRIENDS AND FAMILY MEMBERS TO TELL MY STORY. I am an ordinary housewife and mother, a nurse by profession—not a professional writer. What gave me the courage to begin writing was my conviction that this was not just my personal story but one strand in the tapestry of Jewish history, including the struggle to create and defend the nation of Israel, and my realization that this great, ongoing story is woven not only from heroic lives but from many ordinary lives like mine.

As you will discover, this story is told in my own unedited voice. I am by turns nostalgic, regretful, hopeful, opinionated. Sometimes I am speaking particularly to my daughter, Dalya; sometimes to Jews throughout the world; sometimes to a much broader audience—to our global community of people of all faiths and beliefs.

May you find in this book some measure of inspiration to continue the struggle for peace in our conflict-ridden world.

Saralea Zohar Aaron
Boston, Massachusetts
June 2009

Editorial Note

In keeping with Jewish tradition, the author has rendered the English word God as G-d throughout this memoir.

INTRODUCTION

THIS IS THE STORY OF THE ODYSSEY OF ONE JEWISH WOMAN FROM A PROVINCIAL AMERICAN TOWN NORTH OF BOSTON TO THE RELIGIOUS MELTING POT OF ISRAEL, TO INDIA, AND BACK TO THE UNITED STATES. Both my fate and my daughter's seem to be intertwined with the destiny of Israel. Perhaps it has been thus ordained.

It was on a clear, warm day in May 1968 that I boarded the Greek cruise liner T.S.S. *Anna Maria,* destined for Israel. I was twenty-five years old, but I had never before traveled abroad. Filled with apprehensions about the sea voyage, with my mother, Ethel, my second stepfather, Eddy, and grandmother, Mama Tzipah, crowding about me, I began to cry uncontrollably. My luggage had already been placed on board and I had the ticket for my cabin. Suddenly, though I knew my cousins would be waiting for me with open arms in Haifa, I got the feeling that my family in America and I might never see each other again. As I sniffled, my stepfather rescued me with a handful of tissues. We all said our goodbyes, I was introduced to my cabin mates—three lovely ladies from Greece— and the ship got ready to disembark.

I soon started to quiet down, especially when my three new roommates tucked me under their wings and included me in their conversation. The first of my roommates in our four-bunk cabin was Mrs. Papanielopoulos, a stout, middle-aged, married woman. Mrs. Veridou and Mrs. Theodoros, her sister, were both widowed, and according to Greek Orthodox custom, they wore black, long-sleeved dresses. They were in their late sixties, and both wore their grayish-black hair neatly pulled back into pugs. Though Mrs. Veridou was quite thin, Mrs. Theodoros was stout. Mrs. Papanielopoulos spoke English well enough to get along, but she and the other two ladies could not write English, so I was appointed their scribe, which I rather enjoyed. All were off to visit with family they had not seen for years in Greece. Mrs. Theodoros insisted that I call her Angie, and she and Mrs. Papas (Mrs. Papanielopoulos told us to feel free to call her that for short, as her son had changed their name to that anyway), and I got on well enough in English. However, Mrs. Veridou spoke no English and I no Greek, so we had to resort to sign language, besides Angie translating for us. Throughout the boat trip these ladies and I had a very good relationship. They taught me basic greetings in Greek, too, which made me a bit more sociable.

Then one day as I was blundering about between the ship's decks trying to find the purser's office, I bumped into a very pleasant lady named Laura Cutter, whose destination was also Israel. Laura was a few years older than I, as well as a bit taller, stocky, with a comely round face, fair skin, glasses, and her dark brown hair done up in a swirl on top of her head. Laura and I decided to team up for the trip. We made a good combo, along with Laura's two elderly cabin mates, both of whom spoke English.

Until we reached Europe, most of the voyage was quite boring, aside from the occasional evening band playing as a Greek male soloist sang along with them. We decided to create our own entertainment, playing cards and strolling back and forth on the decks in the evening, with Laura and I walking arm-in-arm followed by our "chaperones," Laura's two cabin mates. The beautiful smell of the ocean was always present. The four of us were excellent company for each other, traveling around Malaga in Spain, Napoli and Pompeii in Italy, Sicily, and ancient Greek ruins, each time the ship stopped to let passengers on and off and to take on cargo.

In Malaga, not only did we get to see a beautifully constructed city with cozy sidewalk cafes and lots of floral decorations, but a city that was spotlessly clean, with all the buildings whitewashed. The people were affable too, and my ability to speak Spanish made the visit more enjoyable. Our tour guide, a very amiable British fellow named Michael, escorted us to a vacant bull ring, where he told us that in Spain bullfighting is still a great art but killing the bull had been outlawed. Our visit to the Lisbon, Portugal, bullring was grim, as we were ushered into the room that is used to hang the carcass of the bull after it has been killed by the matador.

Next, stopping off at Napoli, Laura and I and other tourists held our breath as we crossed the street, as the cars seemed to be going sixty miles an hour, with no traffic lights and no hand signals. The medieval architecture and cathedrals were beautiful there, with their steeples and towers soaring into the sky.

At the ruins of Pompeii, twice destroyed by eruptions from Mount Vesuvius many hundreds of years ago, Laura and I took pictures of the exquisite mosaic and tiled floors that remained. We also got to see the closed plumbing systems which the Pompeiians had constructed in their well-built stone shops and homes, some with as many as five rooms. We were also shown finely made gold and other jewelry and pottery that had remained intact after the molten lava flow had destroyed the city. The Pompeiians had quite a flourishing civilization in their day.

In sad contrast though, as we arrived with our tour group in Sicily, was the poverty in which the local people lived. A young boy, barefoot and in tattered rags, stooped over, cupped his hands, and drank water from a gutter where a horse had just been. Some people begged for alms, and each of us gave them some money. Several Sicilians offered us rides in their horse-drawn carriages for a small fee, but Laura and I decided instead to take pictures of each other posing with the horses and carriages.

After leaving Sicily our ship stopped at Athens, a beautiful European city combining the modern with the old, where we bought a number of well-made dolls of men and women in native Greek attire for good prices. Then it was off by bus to the Acropolis atop a huge hill. There were incredibly well preserved temples to the goddess Athena and the god Apollo at the Parthenon (whose name is derived from the word for virgin, referring to the goddess Athena). Though only the bases and columns of the Parthenon remained, the view was breathtaking, and one needed to use only a little of one's imagination to envision how it must have looked with the Greek priests and priestesses in it twenty-five hundred years ago. We could see for miles around, to the surrounding countryside and towns, as well as to the Mediterranean Sea, from the Acropolis. Laura and I found it very interesting, as we listened to our Greek guides, to hear of their great reverence for the ancient Greek deities—apparently greater than their reverence for their current Greek Christian Orthodoxy. It did not seem totally incongruous though. In view of the Greek culture having been steeped in mythology for over two millennia, it is not strange that Greek deities and Christianity should be valued side by side.

As for the rest of the cruise, it was made enjoyable by delicious food, a couple of captain's cocktail parties, and several "dance-along" parties with Greek, Israeli, and other international dancing that everyone participated in, some of us learning as we danced. The ship's crew was very accommodating, and the facilities were kept very clean. Most of the cruise was smooth sailing, except on one occasion, when the ship went off course a bit to get to Portugal faster for cargo delivery, and we all got seasick. This lasted only a few hours fortunately, without further incident, so that, all told, the trip was really enjoyable. My roommates and I parted as dear friends when the T.S.S. *Anna Maria* docked at Piraeus, Greece. To our regret, we would be unable to carry on a correspondence, as they could not write in English, and I could not write in Greek. Nevertheless, we embraced and wished each other all the best. Laura and I kept each other good company for the last five days of the trip.

After we reached Israel, many were the days when Laura and I went window shopping, or more correctly, stall shopping, in East Jerusalem, sometimes purchasing garments we needed or gifts for the families back home (Laura's home was in Canada). We would occasionally stop at a coffee shop there and just take in the multi-ethnic sights as we had our coffee.

We had a couple of delightful visits with old friends of Laura's, the Sepelians, an Armenian family who lived in East Jerusalem, with a lovely garden surrounding the entrance to the house. The inside of the Sepelians' home consisted of several small but nicely decorated rooms, with the end tables and main dining room table covered with finely crocheted doilies and a tablecloth that Mrs. Sepelian had crocheted herself, and with bowls of fruits and nuts on the tables. Laura and I were treated to cups of Turkish coffee and Middle Eastern pastry as we chatted with the Sepelians. The family were well educated, and Mrs. Sepelian's daughter was an anesthesiologist at the Victoria Augusta Hospital. The family all spoke excellent English. Mrs. Sepelian had short, gray hair and glasses—and a sharp sense of humor. She used to say, "Someday there will be another world flood, as in the days of Noah, and at the end the only ones left will be Armenians."

Laura and I formed a strong friendship during our travels, although she was aware of my strong feelings of Jewishness, as I was of her deep feelings about Christianity. We never intruded into each other's beliefs or way of life. She and I corresponded after we left Israel, but when I got married five years later we agreed to part company, as Laura was a missionary, which was unacceptable to my husband. Laura was a true friend to me, as she said that my marriage should come first, even if it meant breaking up our friendship. I shall not forget her integrity.

ONE

FAMILY LEGACIES

MY FAMILY HERITAGE ON THE MATERNAL SIDE WAS DERIVED FROM THE HASIDIC JEWS OF RUSSIA. This family came from a village called Korosk, in Valiner Gebernia—Gebernia meaning province. It was like the concept of the *shtetl* (village) in Yiddish. The family maintained a very reserved existence among a few other Jewish families, surrounded by Russians and in constant fear of attacks by gypsies and Cossacks. When the gypsies came, you did not stand in their way, as they literally twisted off the geese's necks and made off with whatever loot they could grab. Their primary interest was usually in stealing animals to eat.

However, this was nothing in comparison with the pogroms. My maternal grandmother, Mama Tzipah, and her sisters—Doni, Toybe, and Anna—told us horror stories of the Cossacks sweeping down on a shtetl on horseback, sabres drawn, to rape and mutilate Jewish women, torture and kill Jewish men, and pillage and then burn entire Jewish communities. There was a time in 1906 that Mama later recalled to my cousin Rachel and me, when, forewarned about a pogrom, our entire family left the house and hid themselves in the cornfields among tall cornstalks. They crouched low when they heard the horses' hooves approaching. As the Cossacks rode by, brandishing their sabres above the heads of our family, Aunt Hannah, in a state of panic, began to scream. Great-grandfather

Benjamin had no choice but to silence her, almost choking Hannah. The Cossacks missed them by inches. On that occasion my family was saved, though other Jewish families were less fortunate, some being slaughtered to the last man, woman, and infant.

Thus, whenever the word was out that Russian soldiers were around, Jewish children were quickly pulled into their houses. Aunt Anna recounted another such story to me, about an incident that occurred one day when she was six years old and decided to take a walk. Her mother, Saralea, for whom I am named, grabbed her, pulled up her dress, and proceeded to spank her soundly for daring to walk about with Russian soldiers in the area.

It was an interesting, bittersweet heritage. My great-grandmother Saralea was married to my great-grandfather Benjamin in a marriage arranged by their parents. Mama Tzipah recounted to me the story her mother had told her of how her engagement party was celebrated. As Saralea and Benjamin sat at either end of a long, wooden table, with twenty-six people sitting between them, Saralea passed an exquisitely crocheted doily through thirteen pairs of hands to Benjamin, as her betrothal gift to him. She was wearing a long, black dress that extended from her neck to her ankles, for propriety. Benjamin was dressed in a dark suit, white shirt, and cravat, and wore a hat, for religious propriety.

The marriage was performed at a later date by an Orthodox rabbi under the Jewish marriage canopy, with Benjamin crushing the wine glass under his foot, to commemorate the destruction of the temple in Jerusalem by the Romans. After the marriage ceremony, as was proper among the Hasidim, Saralea's head was completely shaven, a wig of plain design placed on her head, and a kerchief placed over the wig and tied very discreetly behind her head, so as to cover her ears also.

Because great-grandma Saralea had lost her mother when she was three years old and never really had a mother figure to turn to, she was at her mother-in-law's mercy, and reaped more than her share of insults. Her husband was also tied to his mother. Nevertheless, they lived a fairly peaceful life of mutual caring and respect, and Saralea bore Benjamin seven children. One of their daughters, Elke, died of tuberculosis in Russia; another, Hannah, died of cancer years later in the United States.

Good medical facilities were scarce in the backwoods of Russia, so children dying of diseases such as scarlet fever, tuberculosis, and dysentery was not uncommon. Fresh citrus fruits were rare, and Mama told us that if one shopped for oranges or lemons in the market, the vendors would ask, "Who's sick in your house?" The basic staples were beets, cabbages, potatoes, beans wheat, and herring, as well as other fish when they were available.

Years later, when I was about five years old and we went through some hard times, we had to eat a gruel made of millet, a somewhat bitter but nutritious grain to which sugar had to be added. Mama Tzipah, Aunt Doni, and my paternal grandmother, Amelia, told us why we should never waste food, reminding us of the locust plagues and starvation they had experienced before coming to America. They told us of many thousands of locusts coming and literally blackening the sky in broad daylight, as they stripped the land bare of every stalk of grain there was. Trying to swat and burn the locusts was to no avail. The cattle starved, and then the people starved.

As people watched their children dying before their very eyes of starvation, they bought, prepared, and cooked rats. Most of Eastern Europe was affected by this locust plague in the early 1900's, my own family knowing of it personally from Russia and Romania, where my paternal grandmother came from, just before sailing to America. My family were among the more fortunate, in that they barely managed to survive on some chickpeas and millet they had stored away in their cellars.

Once, years later, when we were living in a housing project in Chelsea, Massachusetts, Mama Tzipah was eating a piece of roast beef while looking out the window. Suddenly a large, brown rat ran by, reminding her of people eating rats in Russia sixty years earlier. Mama vomited on the spot. For the rest of her life, Mama Tzipah ate only chicken and fish, along with fruits, vegetables and dairy products. The memory of rats eaten in time of starvation never left her.

As for education in Russia, Jewish girls were given a limited education in Yiddish, mostly for prayers, while the boys, including Uncle Joseph, the only boy in the family, attended a one-room Hebrew school. This was taught by a learned, itinerant Jew who was put up by various Jewish families in the shtetl. My Uncle Joe excelled in his studies and was given a prize of his own copy of the Scriptures in Hebrew, as first boy in the class.

Uncle Joe was an impressive man—six feet tall, with a balding head of light brown hair, an aquiline nose, compassionate blue eyes, a potbelly, and a slightly hoarse voice. His great love of education and his appreciation of the literary classics, as well as the musical classics of Rubinstein, Beethoven, and Bach, he imparted to me from childhood. He had been an accountant, an authority on classical records, and fluent in six different languages. He never married, but Uncle Joe lavished much love on me and my daughter, as well as on his other nieces and nephews.

As the locust plagues, hunger, and pogroms worsened, my family made the decision to go to America, packed their possessions, and in 1903 sailed for the "Golden Medina" (Golden Land). After a dreadful trip, during which the ship hit a great rock and almost capsized, and the captain asked everyone to get on his knees and pray to G-d, the ship managed to make it to New York and then Boston. From there, our family headed for Chelsea. There the least literate of the newcomers settled on Second Street, which later became known as Chelsea's "skid row." From that skid row location were to come some of the country's finest teachers, barristers, and musicians. In those days it was family dignity, hard work, and study that made you tick, not street location. Later the family branched off to other streets in Chelsea and elsewhere for residence. Nevertheless, as far as the Golden Country was concerned, the illusion was soon broken, as my Aunt Doni had to go to work sixteen hours a day in a sweat shop at age fourteen, and the rest of the family worked their fingers to the bone as well.

A great deal of credit was given my great-grandma Saralea, by all who knew her, for her decision to better herself and her family by learning English at night school. This was in addition to all the usual household chores of cooking, washing, baking, sewing, and shopping. This was in the days before washing and drying machines, when most work had to be done by hand. She also maintained the family leadership when great-grandpa Benjamin died at age fifty-four, just before the Hebrew Passover, the most important family holiday on the Hebrew calendar. Despite her loss, she kept both the spirit and the *kashruth* (kosher) tradition, not only for that Passover but for all others as long as she lived.

Everyone came to her for pearls of wisdom on family matters, and for religious blessings. From the pictures that remain of her, together with the rest of the family just before embarking for America, she was an exceptionally attractive woman. She had an oval face, straight nose, and lovely arched eyebrows framing her soft, hazel eyes over thin, well-shaped lips. Her brown hair was combed straight back, tucked under her dark shawl. A charcoal-sketched portrait of her done a few years before she died showed a woman whose eyes were deeply thoughtful, reflecting the agonies she had suffered during her life, having buried her husband and two children. There was a special serenity about her face, though, with her gray hair pulled into a pug at the back of her head. That portrait is one of my most treasured possessions.

Great-grandma Saralea lived to be seventy-seven. Mama Tzipah told me of the great remorse she had felt when, hearing that her mother was near the end, she ran as fast as she could to fetch her daughter Ethel from school in a bitter frost. Upon arriving at the nursing home, she was tearfully told by Aunty Toybe, "It's too late. There's no one to see any more." She cried intensely whenever she reminded herself of that day. All of Chelsea's ethnic groups turned out in throngs at the funerals, respectively, of great-grandpa Benjamin, and then later of great-grandma Saralea.

The story of my family's second great matriarch, Mama Tzipah (Tziporah in Yiddish), who raised me and to a lesser extent my cousins Rachel and Richard, now needs to be told. From the time of her marriage to her late husband, Abraham, she had had a difficult life. Though he had been a machinist, he was never much of a wage earner. Thus, after giving birth to two daughters, my grandmother found herself working hard as a ward aide in the Chelsea Memorial Hospital, a place where I would also work four decades later. Mama Tzipah (as she was like a mother to me) went out to work on occasional confining cases, too, to make ends meet. At one point she developed a blood clot in her leg and was herself confined to bed for many weeks.

The wear and tear of the hardships she endured during her younger years was very evident, as at age fifty-four Mama looked more like a woman of seventy, with a wrinkled face and stooped shoulders. This was in great contrast to how she looked in the family picture taken shortly before they sailed for America, when she was eighteen years old. In that picture Mama was tall, with a good figure, her fine facial features resembling her mother's, all framed by a full updo of dark auburn hair. She was dressed, as were most of the women, in an ankle-length, high-collared, long-sleeved dark dress of plain cotton.

My maternal great-grandparents, Saralea and Benjamin Swiatez, and their children, in about 1903, before leaving the Ukraine for the United States. Seated, left to right: Saralea, Anna, Benjamin. Standing: Joseph, Donya (Doni), Hannah, Tziporah (Mama Tzipah), Toybe.

Though she never learned much English (Mama Tzipah could read the headlines in the local papers, but a detaching retina prevented her from reading the smaller print), she tried her best to improve on it. There was a humorous incident she told us about stemming from her first weeks in America. One day some friends took her to see a movie. A shop owner was placing a hat pin through the actress's hat and Mama let out a shout in Yiddish: *"Oivay, zai shtechen eer arain noodlen in kop!"*—which translated into English was "They're sticking needles into her head." Her girlfriends explained what had really happened and gradually got her to calm down. Thus began Mama Tzipah's Americanization.

There was another incident, though less humorous, that Mama Tzipah told us about from her early days in America. She and her cousin Raizel's sister, also a new immigrant, both of whom were very near-sighted, got jobs in a Jewish restaurant. One day they were asked to deliver soup to a table and they didn't notice a match in one of the plates. As the customer complained angrily, the chef shouted at the two frightened waitresses in Yiddish, *"Dee tvai blinda choorkes, es iz du a shvaibl in yuchi."* Translated, that meant, "You two blind devils, there's a match in the soup!" Of course Mama Tzipah and her cousin rushed to replace the soup plate, but the experience had been upsetting.

To return to Mama Tzipah's bringing us up, she knew the value of a good education and saw to it that we went to school regularly. Though she was slowly going blind, Mama spoke with my teachers often in broken English, and she made me a surprise birthday cake and party at school every year till junior high school. She saw to it that I was properly dressed, though our finances were limited, and took my cousins and me to the Chelsea Public Library for free-of-charge movies. We did not realize until years later that Mama had often deprived herself of food to make sure that we ate. There is much to be said for grandparents who stand by their families when the chips are down. From such elders come rich family heritages and rich communities.

There was a lot of fun and good old-fashioned Yiddish humor that also went into that upbringing. I remember the time when I was eight years old and Mama was teaching me how to knead dough. I made the consistency of the dough too loose, and Mama commented in Yiddish (translated here), "That dough isn't even thick enough to paste up a cat's eyes with it." Now, why in heaven's name anyone would want to paste up a poor cat's eyes is beyond me, but thus went the Yiddish expression.

Then there was the time when Mama Tzipah and I were at the dry cleaner's and were not quite out the door. Mama commented in Yiddish about the proprietor, a very stout, dark-complected woman, who had just dyed her hair platinum blonde and put it up in a French twist, (translated into English), "It suits her like a garland of flowers on a pig." As I barely controlled my laughter, all I could think of was a huge pig, standing in a puddle of mud, with a large garland of flowers on top of its head.

To backtrack a bit, though this humorous situation occurred years before I was born, Mama Tzipah told it to me so well that I could almost see the story happening before my eyes. When Mama was first married, people used iceboxes, as there was no refrigeration yet, and ice was delivered on a daily basis. Mama had a Jewish iceman who had an excessive secretion of saliva, and was also plagued by a wife and two daughters who were very unkind to him. He had found in Mama an empathetic listener, so he told her his tales of woe.

As she retold it to me, it went something like this. "Tzipah, my wife and two daughters are so miserable to me (slurp) that if it weren't for my son-in-law, Gershon (slurp), I wouldn't even have enough money to buy myself a cravat (slurp). They're so terrible to me that I don't even have money to go to a movie (slurp), except that Gershon gives it to me, bless his soul (slurp). Life is so awful (slurp, slurp), Tzipah, I'm fed up." As the iceman's tales of woe went on and on, the huge cake of ice on the leather pad on his back dripped all over the floor. Invariably, each time that the iceman came (which was every day, except on weekends), there would be a new tale of woe, with Mama being a good listener, and with the floor needing to be repeatedly mopped dry from the ice cake drippings. Stories like these were told in a style rooted in the Yiddish tradition of slapstick comedy that was devoid of any affectation and often helped make life, especially in unpleasant situations, much more bearable.

As for Mama Tzipah's Passover meals, they were almost as superb as Aunty Anna's (to be described a little later on). From age sixty till she was eighty years old, she always cleaned and filleted ten pounds of fish, from which she prepared *gefilte* fish, made from fish seasoned and stuffed with carrots, onions, parsley, and garlic and baked until tender. She also cooked a carrot *tzimmes,* made of several pieces of beef, onions, and prunes, plus a little potato starch, a potato, and well seasoned with salt, pepper, and garlic, together with about a pound and a half of carrots, all cooked to a thick consistency. Then Mama prepared a potato *kugel* (raw, finely grated potatoes, seasoned and mixed with beaten eggs and grated onions and baked till brown). The customary dried fruits, nuts, Passover cake (which Mama baked), and coffee followed. Grandma Amelia and Uncle Saul, some family friends, and I attended the first Passover *seder*, while Cousins Rachel and Harvey, and their children, Eric and Bonnie attended the second seder (which I attended, too).

Due to my allergy to fish, I was unable to enjoy Mama Tzipah's gefilte fish, but I thoroughly enjoyed all the other delicacies. Mama delighted in serving us seconds and thirds. Whenever I wasn't working, I pitched in to help with Mama's seder preparations. Neighbors came from down the street to compliment Mama on the aromas of her seder meal preparations.

Mama Tzipah lived with my mother, Ethel, and me, first on Chestnut Street and later in a housing project in Chelsea, until 1970, when my cousins Rachel and Harvey took her to live with them. She remained with them for the next fourteen years as an important member of the household. (The housing project had become too uncivilized a place for her to live.) My daughter, Dalya, and I

Mama Tzipah, at 77.

visited with her at their house in Quincy, and Mama sometimes came to stay with us for a little holiday. (Her husband had died many years earlier of asthma.) She spent the last two weeks of her life under our roof, her body racked by severe degenerative arthritis, among other maladies.

During the last two days of her life, Mama suddenly began to speak English almost exclusively, though she had spoken mostly Yiddish the rest of her life, and called to all of our departed relatives, one by one.

She called to her late mother and to her sister, Hannah, who had died fifty years earlier from cancer, as well as to my Uncle Saul, who had died recently. She called to them over and over again, after she had finished calling to my cousin, Rachel, and me. It was as if she were preparing to meet with our departed relatives shortly.

As the life drained slowly from her body, Mama Tzipah asked only for ginger ale, and as a last resort to nourish her, I tried feeding her some blueberry yogurt. This would be the last thing I fed her while she was still conscious. Her last words to me, as I fed her, were in English: "I'll remember you." I bathed and changed Mama, as she had done innumerable times for Rachel and Richard and me when we were small, and she slowly lapsed into unconsciousness on June 10, 1985.

That evening Mama Tzipah went to sleep in a realm where there were no more pogroms, no more famine, no more inhumanity of man to man, and no more deprivation, of which she had known so much in her lifetime. She had gone to join her mother and father and the rest of our ancestors, to be at peace forever after. Mama had lived a full life, full of dedication to her family, and died in dignity, with her sisters, Doni and Toybe, at her side shortly before she died, and with my daughter, Dalya, and me with her till the end. As she died, I rent my garments, according to the tradition of grieving in the Hebrew faith, and said a prayer for the dead. About fifty people attended the funeral, including "Uncle" Ralph Hensey (my "honorary uncle"), for he was as immediate family as anyone. After the funeral he held me tenderly in his arms, telling me what a fine eulogy I had given Mama. Unbeknown to him or to me, his own death was to follow shortly after that.

One of the several other rich legacies from the maternal side of my family was contributed by Mama's sister, Aunty Toybe. Her oval face, framed by black, wavy hair pulled back loosely into a pug, often wore a somber expression, but her visits to our house on Chestnut Street were greatly anticipated, as she always brought something for everyone, including a new, exciting story book for me. One of her deepest concerns was for abused animals, and she instilled those feelings into Dalya and me, too. Once when she was in her early seventies, I went to look after her, as she was ill. It was in the midst of a severe frost, and the ground was covered with ice. Aunty Toybe insisted that I take a large bag of bread out to feed the birds. I am also a lover of animals, but I was not inclined to go out to an ice-covered yard to fall and get hurt. Nevertheless, she was so fearful that the birds would starve, that I did as she asked, though I almost fell several times. If I were paid a thousand dollars to do that again, I think I would refuse to do it.

Aunty Toybe's daughter, Voltairine, sometimes got tickets for Mama Tzipah and me to go to Boston's Symphony Hall to attend the children's concerts. That was my first exposure to the wonderful musical world of Foster, Wagner, Tchaikovsky, and many other great composers. Voltairine was herself an accomplished musician who played the flute, piano, and guitar. She used to conduct a children's radio program on station WCOP, as she played the piano. She was very sensitive with children, smiling at them with her beautifully dimpled face and dark eyes, all framed, like her mother's, by jet black, wavy hair. Unfortunately, Voltairine died childless, after marrying late in life to Alef (his nickname), a very fine gentleman and professor of medicine, from Afghanistan.

Aunty Toybe's younger sister, Aunty Doni, was the perfect homemaker, with every piece of furniture and every plant in its place. We used to look forward to her delicious "moon *korjes*" (hard poppyseed cookies) when we visited with her. She also made terrific spinach *borscht* (dairy soup, with potatoes and sour cream). I can still picture Aunty Doni leaning over the stove, her aquiline nose, like Uncle Joe's, complementing her oval face, with her grayish black hair pulled into a pug at the back of her neck. She wore an all-encompassing apron, tied with a neat bow in the back. She always spoke her piece, direct and to the point.

The great event of the year until about fifty years ago was the Passover seder celebrated by the entire family at the Brookline home of Aunty Anna (the youngest of Mama Tzipah's sisters) and Uncle Abe. All the sisters and the one brother of Aunty Anna, the children, grandchildren, and many cousins came for this most special Jewish holiday. Many of the women would arrive well in advance of the seder hour, going into the kitchen to help Aunty Anna get things ready. The oldest women, including Mama Tzipah, Cousin Frima (who always had a twinkle in her eye), Cousin Freda (who baked the most fantastic *chalah*), and Miss Kirk, Aunty Anna's dear old friend from nursing school days, would huddle in the left side of the parlor. They would reminisce about how Passover was celebrated years ago, in great-grandma Saralea's little wooden house in Valiner, with everything prepared tediously over the wood stove, by hand.

At the same time the men of the family would gather at the right side of the parlor to discuss politics, the economy, and the current state of affairs in Israel. We younger cousins could hardly wait for the discussions, and for the reading of the *Haggadah* (the story of the Exodus of the Jews from Egypt) to be over with, so that we could eat all of the delicious food Aunty Anna had prepared, plus see which one of us would receive the *afikoman*, the hidden middle part of *matzoh* (unleavened bread) that has a gift to go with it. During the seder the reading of the Haggadah went around the table, with each one of us reading a portion.

The youngest children read the four questions of the Passover, whose responses included the reasons for eating unleavened bread, the eating of bitter herbs to remind us of the bitterness of bondage by the Egyptians, the eating of a mixture of crushed nuts, wine, and cinnamon to remind us of the mortar we had to use to build Pharaoh's monuments, and all the other significant events that the seder symbolized.

Then came the Passover feast. In addition to the matzoh and wine (accompanied by blessings), and soup with matzoh balls, Aunty Anna roasted a mouth-watering turkey, served with carrot tzimmes. Abundant plates of dried fruits followed, plus scrumptious Passover sponge cakes, served with coffee. Of course, there were also Passover macaroons, chocolates, and candied fruit rings to follow the dinner. No one ever came away hungry from Aunty Anna's table. It would have been a physical impossibility, especially at Passover.

I can still envision Aunty Anna, slightly stocky and short, with her auburn hair done in an Italian cut, her round, pretty face accented by fashionable dark-framed glasses, scurrying around the kitchen, tending to every last detail for the seder. I believe that no one could have outdone Aunty Anna in preparing from scratch the most palate-whetting dishes. For her it was a work of love, as it delighted her to see the look of wonderment and relish, especially on the grandchildren's faces.

Uncle Abe also took great pride in helping Aunty Anna prepare for the seders. He would be bending over the kitchen counter, cutting up vegetables, with his handsome, round face and a full head of wavy brown hair set above cheerful brown eyes, also set with glasses. Between tasks, he and Aunty Anna would hug one grandchild and then another, as they ran up to them. The children of the family were their delight.

There was another, deeply traditional reason for the big Passover celebrations at Anna and Abe's house every year. Great-grandma Saralea had lived for the last few years of her life in their house, and had set the precedent for a very pious and meaningful Passover there. Thus, after she passed away, Passovers were celebrated very much in great-grandma Saralea's tradition. I am honored that some of her culinary and other relics have been passed down to me. To this day I carefully guard an old copper pot in which she used to cook fish for the Sabbath in Russia, plus her old soup pot, and a pair of old brass candelabra which she had used to bless the Sabbath candles when she stayed over at Aunty Toybe's and her late husband Uncle Asher's home years ago. These relics will be passed down for my daughter and her children to cherish and honor after me. The memories that I have of all of us together since fifty years ago at Aunty Anna and Uncle Abe's house for these occasions will be treasured forever. Both Anna and Abe died in the past thirteen years, after having led full lives and gone through serious illnesses.

On the paternal side of the family, our grandparents came from the villages of Fokshynee and Botershynee in Romania. My paternal grandmother's mother died at a young age, unfortunately, so that Grandma Amelia's Aunt Leah ended up bringing up the four children, as well as tending to their father. After a marriage was arranged between Grandmother Amelia and Grandfather Abraham, they decided to try their fortune in America, where some cousins were already established. The going was rough, though. After arriving in the United States, and after staying awhile with the cousins and having a child on the way, they had to rent a place of their own, and ended up in Chelsea.

Of course, birth control was essentially unthought of in those days, and our grandparents had four children in rapid succession. This was not a problem in itself, except that Grandfather Abraham suddenly developed a leaking heart valve, for which there was no treatment then, and died before the age of thirty. The public assistance was limited in those days, so Grandmother Amelia supported her brood by scrubbing floors and sometimes caring for a private family after a mother gave birth. I recall her vividly telling us how bad she felt when the children asked her to take them out to a restaurant. Her bright idea was to pack up a bag of homemade cookies or cakes, order a cheap drink, and spread her items out on the restaurant table on the cloth table napkin she'd brought from home. When the waitress came along and said, "I'm sorry, Madam, but you can't do that—you have to order food here," Grandma put her directly in her place with the snapping retort, "I haven't any money! That's all!" Angry and confused, the waitress walked away! Our family ate and drank their refreshments from home and left. In that way they got to eat out.

I can imagine what the restaurant scene looked like. Grandma Amelia, short and stocky, with an attractive, fair face, dark brown eyes, and flaming red, wavy hair, had a lovely smile. However, when she was in a bad mood she would instinctively put on such a severe scowl that her face seemed twisted out of shape.

Grandma Amelia tasted more than her share of bitterness, though, when she lost her daughter, Ruth (for whom my husband and I later named our daughter, though years later she had her name legally changed to Dalya). Ruth died after complications from a tonsillectomy at Boston's Children's Hospital. Aunt Ruth was known as one of the most charitable souls, and when she got money gifts she told Grandma to give them to a less fortunate family. Aunt Ruth died when she was fifteen years old.

Some years later, Grandma Amelia's son, Israel, and Mama Tzipah's daughter, Ethel, met and married in Chelsea, and settled down there. That was how Chelsea came to be my hometown, when I arrived on the scene a couple of years later. I was given the great honor of being named after great-grandma Saralea. This is according to Hebrew tradition. As fortune would have it, I was an only child and was introverted, so that I did not make friends easily. I had a stuffed toy dog named Dixie, and every night before I went to sleep I read stories to Dixie. I kept Dixie until I was about ten years old and then lost it.

Notwithstanding my having been basically a loner, I had two close girlfriends till I was about ten years old, Ruthie Greenspan and Mary Boroian. (I shall refer to Mary in the next chapter, as to how her family and ours met.) They were two of the wildest tomboys, and taught me how to be a tomboy, too. We three used to climb up the walls of the Chelsea Post Office, up over the window ledges, and then wait for any sailors to walk by on the sidewalk below, and jump over their heads. Of course, as we did so and they gave chase to us, we ran away lickety-split into the bushes behind the Post Office, and didn't get caught.

However, there was one time when the three of us decided to climb up the hill of Bellingham Street and steal flowers from a garden that had a "No Trespassing" sign on it. As we grabbed a flower and ran, Ruthie and Mary managed to jump over the short fence and get away, but I didn't. A very tall, angry young woman rushed out of the house, grabbed me by the arm, admonished me sternly, and scared the daylights out of me. Ruthie and Mary tried to console me, but the thought of the tall, young woman grabbing and shaking me did not easily leave my mind. We had to find some less hazardous trouble to get into the next time.

That was in the late 1940's, at about the time that the Tobin Bridge (named for the late governor of Massachusetts, Maurice Tobin, and more commonly referred to as the Mystic River Bridge) was just being erected, part of it right behind our house on Chestnut Street. Nearly all of our houses had back porches on them, and from there we watched the massive excavations that were going on in the area. We got a thrill out of watching huge brown and gray rats come scurrying out of their dens, and Ruthie, Mary, and I had our fun playing in the excavation sites. We watched the neighborhood cats chasing and catching the rats, and we built mud houses from the excavation material.

This wasn't enough excitement though, and so one evening Mary and I decided to stuff lima beans, bubble gum, and toilet paper up both sides of our noses to see what would happen. We did this in the back room of our Chestnut Street apartment and started to choke. Mama was partially blind at this time, and started to panic as she saw us in this state. She called Dr. Berson, who was my pediatrician, and he told Mama to have Mary and me sniff in some Soapine, a popular household soap powder at the time. Bit by bit we began to sneeze out the sticky material, till it all came out. Then we got our punishment from Mama and Almas Boroian—a few good whacks on our bottoms and no chocolates for the rest of the week. I now sit back and wonder how our poor grandmothers and mothers ever managed to put up with three wild animals such as Ruthie, Mary, and I were in those days.

There is one last amusing experience during my childhood that is worth mentioning. This involved Grandma Amelia in the kitchen, when she still lived on Congress Avenue, not far from the center of Chelsea. Grandma had been given a pressure cooker pot to facilitate cooking for the family. Unfortunately, Grandma Amelia had not gotten all the exact instructions as to how to operate the pressure cooker, and forgot that once the pot came near to boiling, she needed to lower the gas flame, and sometimes remove the pressure release gadget on top completely. Thus, one fine day after Grandma had put some beef with potatoes, lima beans, and onions to cook in the pressure cooker, and got to work sorting out laundry with me at the back of the house, she forgot that she had left the pot on a moderately high flame with the release gadget still on. Suddenly an explosive sound came blasting out from the kitchen, and lo and behold, the top of the pressure cooker had blown off, with the contents of partially cooked meat, potatoes, beans, and onions plastered all over the ceiling and walls adjacent to the stove. The rest of it had descended on top of the stove, with some of it having hit the floor upside down. What a time we had, cleaning up the ceiling with a mop held upside down; and after work, poor Uncle Saul having to borrow a neighbor's step ladder to climb up the kitchen walls with a pile of wet rags and scrub off the food that had gotten stuck there. Believe it or not, there still was enough food left in the pressure cooker for the three of us to get a meal out of it. However, from that time on Grandma Amelia gave up using the pressure cooker, and decided to go back to the old-fashioned way of cooking with ordinary pots with lids on them.

Apparently, certain items of modernization have not been meant for all of us. In this case, the pressure cooker was definitely not meant for Grandma Amelia, though she was a very good cook otherwise, with her lamb and split pea soup having been second to no one's, as well as her delicious noodle puddings.

To return briefly to the story of the Tobin Bridge, its construction had one very sad result: the destruction of many fine old houses that had lined the city from the U.S. Naval Hospital, bordering the Mystic River at Chelsea's most southern point, up to Fourth Street, which was about in the middle of Chelsea. It was the harbinger of what was to follow seven years later, with the construction of the Northeast

Expressway, which caused the demolition of half of Jefferson Avenue, probably Chelsea's finest street, just beyond the city's Prattville section. Eventually, much more than half of Jefferson Avenue was torn down for that project. Chelsea then became known as "the transportation mecca of New England."

TWO

CHELSEA, MY HOMETOWN

As for the rest of my childhood, I was brought up in a cosmopolitan environment in Chelsea, speaking mostly Yiddish. I was also exposed to Polish, Russian, and Armenian, and to the cultures of most of these ethnic groups. In regard to our friendship with the Boroians, we met in the small park near the Williams School when I was four years old. Almas Boroian was there with her children, Michael, four years older than I, Mary, who was four, and Martin, who was then two. Almas spoke mostly Armenian and broken English, and was quite poor; Mama Tzipah spoke mostly Yiddish and broken English and had little money, so already they had a lot in common.

Almas and Mama Tzipah started up a conversation while watching over us and decided to become friends. Almas and her children then lived with her husband, more than twenty years her senior, very domineering and unkind, the result of an arranged marriage in Armenia. They lived on Everett Avenue, about four blocks down from us, and we often went to interesting places together, bringing food from home. Considering the delicious food that Almas and Mama cooked, why bother to eat out anyway, even if we had the money?

A big festivity to look forward to every summer was the Armenian picnic-concerts at Maynard, Massachusetts, to which the Boroians took us. The melodies still resound in my ears, as I recall the men, women, and children all dancing in a circle to the music of violins, flutes, tambourines, and finger cymbals. Armenian and most Middle Eastern music is in the minor key and harmoniously repetitive. At those concerts the aromas of pilaf and shish kebab permeated the flower- and forest-scented air—a welcome change from the foul air of the Chelsea Creek at low tide. The family unity and respect for elders shown by the Boroians, Avedisians, and everyone else was a heartwarming expression of the dignity and familial strength of the Armenian people.

As for what became of the Boroians, Michael acquired a position on the state police force, where I believe he remained. Mary married and had children, though unfortunately not the kind of marriage Almas would have wanted for her. Martin had quite an academic brain, and was supposed to have gone to a school of higher education after public school. As for Almas herself, she would be in her eighties now, wherever she may be. May G-d keep them all well; they were like our own family.

A word needs to be mentioned now about the housing we had. Most of Chestnut Street consisted of red brick buildings, with a few wooden three-story houses interspersed every now and then. My parents were divorced when I was four, so my mother, Ethel, Mama Tzipah, and I occupied a four-room apartment on the first floor of a red brick, three-story building. I remember it had a gray, wooden back porch where we hung out our clothes to dry, and a vegetable storage place in the back hall, which led to the porch. There was an oil burner in the kitchen, which provided both the cooking and the heating for the apartment. Oil burners were the most common means of providing central heating in those days. Landlords also supplied their tenants with boilers in their kitchens, which furnished hot water.

We had some floral wallpaper on our parlor and bedroom walls, and our hardwood floors were covered with linoleum. Unfortunately, the apartment also had some guests that we had never invited: cockroaches, which were all over the walls and ceilings. At one point as we were seated at the table, a large roach fell off the ceiling onto a tablespoon of gruel that Izzy (my father, Israel), who had been very abusive to us, was about to put into his mouth. From then on, when Izzy was at the table and saying something nasty to us, we would ask him, "Would you like a cockroach with your gruel?" Whenever we, our middle-floor neighbors, or our third-floor neighbors sprayed, the roaches migrated and returned.

The Piontaks, a Polish-American family, lived next door to us. Every day, when the sun was out, we would see the elderly Mr. Piontak, a widower, carefully tending to his flower garden, which he kept fenced in around the house. His neatly arranged beds of roses, violets, tulips, and other plants brightened up the city block. Mr. Piontak's two daughters, who did secretarial work, always had a pleasant word for us. Mama Tzipah got along just fine with Mr. Piontak, as she spoke Polish fluently. The O'Briens, who lived across the street from us, were less desirable neighbors. They often got into quarrels with us and the other neighbors when their son and his friends played ball right against our windows.

At one point Grandma Amelia and Uncle Saul moved into an apartment in one of the wooden houses on Chestnut Street, just a few houses down the street from us. They then had two dogs, a white Maltese terrier named Nelly and a small, black mongrel named Princess. We were all dog lovers, and I used to love to play with Nelly and Princess every chance I had. The dogs took naturally to Mama Tzipah, too.

A couple of doors up the street lived one of Mama's best friends, Annie Shankel, a short, stocky Jewish lady with a kerchief perpetually on her head. She lived there with her husband and one unmarried daughter (the older daughter already having married and moved out). I distinctly remember Annie's kitchen as always being very hot, as she was always cooking or baking something. My great delight there, as Annie and Mama Tzipah chatted away, was in savoring one of Annie's' delicious sour pickles or sour tomatoes. And the sub shops think they have something special to offer us now!

As our house was within about a five-minute walk from Chelsea Square, Mama Tzipah would often take my cousin Rachel and me for walks through the park, which was in the center of the Square, and the shops on either side of Broadway. There was a florist shop on the corner, followed by Craft's men's wear and an all-purpose camping supplies store. Dalis's Caterers followed Craft's, a barbershop, and a few other stores. Across the street from the florist's was a pharmacy; just beyond that the world-renowned Chelsea Clock Company, and a furniture store. On the next block was the Chelsea Police Station, with the Court House adjacent to it. Behind the Police Station was the Winnissimmett Yarn Shop, to which the women would flock from many communities for its unique supply of yarns and all manner of needlework materials. It was fun going through Chelsea Square in the 1950's.

Those were the happy days, but happiness does not go on forever, and my first serious exposure to death, when I was seven years old, was the passing of my Uncle Sunya, Aunty Doni's husband. He was in his mid-sixties, not an old age by current standards. Whenever Mama Tzipah and I had visited with Aunty Doni and Uncle Sunya, he was bubbling over with love, holding me, as well as his own grandchildren, on one of his knees, telling us stories in Yiddish or in English. He had an ability to look into people's souls and determine their characters. Shortly after Uncle Sunya's death, one night when I was tucked away in bed with Mama, I suddenly got up, crying and hugging Mama with all my might, sobbing that I was afraid she would die, too. Mama handled it very maturely, hugging me in turn, and explaining to me that someday everybody has to die, but that she didn't expect to die for quite some time to come. It took her a couple of hours to console me, and then I finally went to sleep alongside of her.

From that time on I became better adjusted to accepting death as a part of life. Thus, when a few years later the time came for Uncle Asher, Aunty Toybe's husband, to die, and a few years after that my first stepfather, Gerry, I was much more prepared to accept it. However, since several years after Pa (Gerry) died, I began questioning more and more why a person so young and so loving as he should have had to die prematurely. Even after having read Rabbi Harold Kushner's book *When Bad Things Happen to Good People,* I continued to ask that question.

That was forty-five years ago, before the second "great conflagration," when Chelsea was still a viable, thriving community, with many synagogues and churches, and a beautiful, Old World shopping area on Arlington Street. (That fire, burned an area of about 18 blocks in 1973; the first, in 1908, burned half the city.) There were large numbers of pushcarts, selling everything from fresh fish to fruits and fabrics, plus several groceries and bakeries, butchers, and delicatessens. I remember the hubbub at our grocer's, the New York Appetizers, run by Sam and Rose Gouchberg, fine hard-working people. There was a blend of Jewish, Italian, Greek, Polish, and Armenian backgrounds, all shopping at this grocery store, speaking a multitude of languages and dialects. From behind the fish and deli meats counter could be heard the gravelly voice of bespectacled Sam Gouchberg, with wavy, black hair combed straight back, shouting orders as to where to put the new shipment of flounder just delivered.

His hoarse-voiced shouting might have made you think that Sam was an angry man, but he was a rather kind man. He always helped poor families by giving them a discount and letting them pay on the installment plan. Rose was always at Sam's side, with her pretty, round face framed by a lofty, blonde coiffure—but you could hear Rose's voice above the din, too, translating for some of the customers in Yiddish and Polish. Sam and Rose were friendly, unpretentious people.

Next to the New York Appetizers was Rosie's Bakery, where I can still recall the aroma of cinnamon and raisins coming from some of the tastiest coffee rolls and Jewish pastries under the sun. Our old, stocky friend, Sylvia, with her boyish bob of black hair in tight ringlets, always managed to sneak a cookie or cupcake to me as a gift, when no one else was looking. To me, up till age eight, that was quite a treat, especially from a warm person like Sylvia.

Then Mama Tzipah and I headed for Mr. Schwachman, the butcher, on Everett Avenue. Slightly stoop-shouldered, white-haired, tall, blue-eyed, and always with a hat on his head (for respect for G-d, according to Judaism), soft-spoken Mr. Schwachman greeted us and all the other customers with a smile. I swear that no other butcher's chickens made as good a soup as his.

Our next stop-off was at Tirck's Pharmacy, where Sam, Harry, and George Tirck greeted us. Sam, with gray hair, wearing glasses, and fairly tall, was the most serious of the three. Next came Harry, short of stature, the family man, with an endless sense of humor. He would talk with Mama on the socio-economic ills of the country at that time. Last but not least came George, the super-intellectual, with his grayish black hair and keenly intelligent eyes. George would sit with Mama at one of the two tables in the drug store and expound on the political situations of the day, one of the worst ills being Senator Joseph McCarthy's policies. We must keep in mind that this occurred sixty years ago, when the cruel, paranoid threat of McCarthyism (labeling people at random as Communists) ruined the lives of many prominent people. George Tirck had a special hatred for

Senator McCarthy, as well as for Judge Irving Kaufman, who sentenced Ethel and Julius Rosenberg to death by electrocution in June of 1953. Judge Kaufman had ordered this sentence for conspiracy in treason (while others were giving atomic secrets to the Soviet Union, also), when a prison term was more in order. The three Tirck brothers were always active in helping fellow Jews in need, and needy people in general. Chelsea was never the same again after the passing of these three saintly pharmacists over thirty-five years ago.

After that was a quick stop-over at rotund Mrs. College's variety store. It was a treat, back in 1952, for us kids to get a plastic tube of multi-colored sugar drops for two cents, plus a big box of animal crackers for ten cents. I smile even now, remembering Mrs. College's cousin's mispronunciation of "Hershey bars," which sounded like a vulgar way of saying horse manure.

On Elm Street, a bit down the road, was the Saievitz family's kosher slaughter house, where Jewish law required not only freshness and cleanliness, but compassion in killing the animals quickly. Whenever a poor Jewish family came by before the Hebrew High Holy Days, Eve Saievitz made sure they got a good portion of meat, often gratis. Diminutive Eve, with her auburn hair done in an updo, would come down from her accounting desk to discreetly tell one of the workers to get a meat order together and hand it to the needy family, as a *mitzvah* (good deed), for the Hebrew New Year. The late Mrs. Abraham Shankman, local head of the Jewish charities, likewise saw to it that every needy Jewish family received food and money for the holy days and through times of hardship. Chelseans used to be like that in those days.

There was much more to Chelsea than that, though. There were several small, fine restaurants back in the fifties, among them Hersom's, which served primarily as an ice cream parlor, with a homey, Continental environment. The Bell-Dell delicatessen specialized in kosher, deli-style food (you could buy a delicious, thick corned beef sandwich for a dollar seventy-five) was at the corner of Chestnut Street and Everett Avenue. There was a similar deli-style restaurant near the corner of Everett Avenue and Arlington Street, and another one on Broadway in Bellingham Square, which was then and still is considered the center of town. These all provided Old World, Jewish-style food. For those catering to the standard

American style of Sloppy Joes, and ham and eggs, there was the Apollo restaurant, also in Bellingham Square. Lastly, there was Wing's restaurant for Chinese-American food, which also had a fine cuisine. It is regrettable that of all these eating-places, only one, Wing's, survived the fires and economic upheavals.

Also on Chelsea's main street, Broadway, were the two movie houses, the Olympia, near Fourth Street, and near Chelsea Square, the cheaper Strand Theater, where the lower income people went. In 1955 we could get in to see a double feature, including one of the finer reruns in Technicolor, such as *Ivanhoe* or *Cinderella,* for the expensive ticket of thirty-five cents there. You brought your own refreshments to the Strand, as well as your own toilet paper and soap, while you could buy popcorn, candy, and soda at the Olympia. Also, at the Strand, air conditioning was provided in summer by opening the theater's front and rear doors. After the movies and maybe an eat-out at Hersom's, on a pleasant summer evening we'd all go to sit and chat on the wooden benches in front of the Post Office.

Summer enjoyment usually meant heading for Revere Beach for swimming and the amusement parks. Pollution as we know it had not yet permeated Revere Beach then. Actually, seventy years ago Chelsea Beach was the place to go, we are told, until the advent of the oil tankers on Marginal Street, when swimmers started coming out of the water covered with oil. Then people started switching to Revere Beach for recreation.

In those days our family lived on Chestnut Street, not far from the Bell-Dell delicatessen, and our upstairs neighbors, the Andruszewskis, were more like family to us. Mrs. Catherina Andruszewski, short, stout, with a slightly wide nose and lips, had sensitive dark brown eyes and her hair done in a page-boy. Her house was always neat as a pin, and notwithstanding her broken English, she had an understanding and love of humanity that many with college degrees could never attain. Mrs. Andruszewski always brought me up to her house to watch television with her children whenever my mother, Ethel, had mental illness attacks. (G-d rest Mrs. Andruszewski's noble soul.) You could smell the aroma of *kielbasa* (Polish sausage) and *kapusta* (meat-stuffed cabbage) wafting out from the open parlor windows of her house

These aromas mingled at Christmas and Chanukah times with the smells of Mama Tzipah's homemade *latkes* (potato pancakes) and *shtrudel*. On those holidays we had wonderful family get-togethers, the Andruszewskis' brightly decorated Christmas tree contrasting, yet harmonizing, with our Menorah, or Chanukah candelabrum, the candles ignited on it to symbolize the triumph of Jews over tyranny many centuries ago. The love of these two ethnically different families was one of the most priceless parts of my childhood heritage. Our families celebrated by bringing our plates of pastries upstairs to the Andruszewski's apartment, while Johnny, Eddie, and Teresa Andruszewski set up tables. Then their sister, Henrietta, would arrive with her husband, Joe, and their two sons. Mama Tzipah, Henrietta, and Catherina would then spontaneously burst into a conversation in Polish, with no lack of comprehension. Stanislaus Andruszewski, well-built but not stocky, with his gray hair combed straight back over his swarthy features, had a smile and hugs for all the grandchildren (me included, of course). He promptly escorted us to the living room to watch television with him, while the women prepared the food. Their conversations included us children, and wishing each other, of course, Merry Christmas and Happy Chanukah and a prosperous New Year. The Andruszewskis and my family spent eleven precious years together.

As children, most of us from that neighborhood attended the Williams School, once known as the biggest school east of the Mississippi River. It was a fine grammar school, and our principal, Mr. Healey, and his wife, who taught second grade, were very caring educators. One person who stands out in my mind from that school was Miss Monaghan, the school superintendent. Notwithstanding her diminutive stature, she was a stern disciplinarian, but also had a great capacity for understanding children. I remember her vividly from my first day at school, as I entered this huge, forbidding-looking red brick building, with the barest knowledge of English, and I began to cry very hard. After trying some unsuccessful communication with me, Miss Monaghan then asked me, "Would you like a dolly?" I replied, "Ya, ya, dolly, dolly." She then led me by the hand into Miss Clark's kindergarten, where I started to mingle with the other students, thanks to Miss Clark's kindness.

Our second grade teacher, Miss Buckley, a woman in her fifties, with severe dark eyes and her gray hair pulled back into a pug, was the opposite of Miss Clark in manner. She believed not so much in praising good students as in scolding students for the smallest infraction. She felt it appropriate to berate a student at the front of the classroom for making noises in the coatroom. On occasion, we would get hit across the knuckles by a ruler if we misbehaved. The more I think of it now, as I hear of students being very fresh with teachers, I think the ruler treatment was not altogether inappropriate.

Within this same context, I remember Miss Brennan, the dancing teacher, criticizing me for a different mistake I made each time we had dancing class. It was a class I came to dread. Miss Whiting, our art teacher, with her Yankee manner, made many of us foreign-speaking students feel very much left out. It wasn't deliberate on her part, but part of her culture.

We must keep in mind that courses in English as a second language did not exist then, and any Greek, Italian, and other foreign-language-speaking children had to struggle it out as best they could. They did so without any special classes for language adaptation. Nowadays, especially since the influx of students from Mexico, Haiti, and Cambodia, special accommodations have been made to ease the transition for those who have used a totally different alphabet. However, the one great asset that my fellow foreign-speaking students and I had was a future ability to become readily multilingual.

I remember one particularly loving teacher, Mrs. Rita Kinsella, our music and Glee Club teacher. I can envision her smiling, round face with her gray hair brushed straight back into a Boyish Bob style, and with a deep but sensitive voice. Mrs. Kinsella always encouraged us to try to feel the emotional tone of the songs we were singing, whether they were Hawaiian Island songs or holiday Christmas and Chanukah songs. She showed obvious pleasure and complimented us when we did a good job. She was never unkind about correcting us. We took great pride in performing for her at Parent-Teacher meetings.

In the fifth grade I acquired two new girlfriends, Carol Miller and Carol Egnit. We lived very close to each other. Notwithstanding the differences in our ethnic backgrounds, as a Jew, an African-American

(Carol Miller), and a Polish-American (Carol Egnit), the three of us had a very good friendship. We all came from the bottom of the socio-economic ladder, so we had lots in common. Carol Miller and I used to go for a piano lesson for fifty cents each week at the school with Mrs. Ida Fine. Mrs. Fine not only gave us excellent lessons, but had a marvelous sense of humor, too. Carol was the more serious student of the two of us. I say with great pride that though the three of us came from homes of deprivation, we were brought up with love and dignity. Carol Egnit's and my grandmothers and Carol Miller's mother saw to it. Special credit was due to Carol Miller's parents, especially her mother, as they had a large family (seven children, I believe), but always taught the children respect for elders, and teachers, and manners. Tragically, Carol Miller's mother died prematurely of heart disease on Thanksgiving Day, when we were in our second year in high school. Carol and I met ten years later, when she was married and had two sons. To my regret, she and Carol Egnit and I have not met since then. We had lots of fun visiting with each other and going to the movies. I sincerely hope that they have fared well.

Digressing back to Chelsea community life, one very important aspect was religion. I remember the synagogues, including Rabbi Twersky's, which was Orthodox, on Chestnut Street, and the Walnut Street and Elm Street synagogues, further down Chelsea, towards the city of Everett, all filled to capacity. There were congregations pouring out into the streets on the High Holy Days, as well as on other holidays. The synagogue our family attended was right across the street from our house and had a homey, Old World atmosphere. In all of these congregations the men and women sat separately, according to Orthodox custom. In the one Conservative synagogue in Chelsea, Temple Emmanuel, both sexes were allowed to sit together. Our family attended Temple Emmanuel after moving to the Locke Street Housing Project in 1954.

The throng of our Polish-American neighbors going to church on Sunday, Christmas, and Easter, was impressive, too, as Chelsea had a large Polish-American population then. The Andruszewskis attended the Saint Stanislaus Church on Chestnut Street, about a block up the street. Others attended the St. Rose Church and other churches in the vicinity, including Protestant and Catholic sects. Jews and Christians alike dressed up for our houses of worship for Holy Days.

Beyond the religious activities, each October the mayor and the Board of Aldermen sponsored a "Parade of Horribles" for Halloween, extending from City Hall to Chelsea Square. There was plenty of fun supervised by adults, with all the youngsters of the community dressed in different costumes. Following the parade was a contest for the three best costumes. The city also provided plenty of punch, cookies, and bobbing for apples. Parents took all the small children out for "trick or treating," without fear of molestation. It was a fun time for all, as it should be.

In addition, Chelsea was quite the center for Independence Day celebrations. Every year on the Fourth of July there was a fantastic display of fireworks after the local dignitaries made their addresses, and the Chelsea High School band played at Carter Ground at the Chelsea Stadium. Just about everyone from Chelsea, and many from Everett, Revere, and East Boston, came especially to see the band play and see the fireworks. It's sad to realize that, unlike the present, in those days everyone felt free to walk all the way home from Carter Ground late at night, without broken beer bottles on the streets. Hundreds of families walked up Everett Avenue with their picnic baskets, taking advantage of the warm, summer night air.

This was the Chelsea that was the home of Horatio Alger, the famed author who wrote hundreds of boys' stories. It was the Chelsea where back in the thirties my mother, among others, played the violin in the famous, winning Conrad Cup Orchestra. It was the Chelsea whose Young Men's and Young Women's Hebrew Association served both the social and the cultural needs of the whole Jewish community. This included a summer camp for the younger children, teenage clubs, a senior citizens group, and a social service office for those with family problems, all services gratis for those who could not afford to pay.

THREE

ADOLESCENCE, CARTER SCHOOL, AND HIGH SCHOOL

To return to the childhood days that my two girlfriends named Carol and I spent together, those were the days when the Chelsea policemen, Officer Swankowski and Lieutenant Holmes, escorted us children across the streets to the Williams and Shurtleff schools with great care. Lieutenant Holmes was the kindest policeman, who cared for us as if we were his own children. He was not a threat, notwithstanding his great height and powerful build, but a friend to look up to in the community.

In 1954 my family moved from Chestnut Street to the Locke Street housing project in Chelsea. There was only one other Jewish family in our project, the Kerner family, who lived across the court from us. We were mutually supportive and celebrated Hebrew holidays together. Among our other good neighbors were the Lombardis, a refined Polish-Italian couple with two lovely daughters, who were confined to the project because of the husband's paralysis. They lived next door to us. Upstairs lived a very pleasant Polish couple, the Naruszewics, who were on in years. Mama Tzipah enjoyed her conversations in Polish with Mrs. Naruszewic when she came down to visit us every so often, and to commiserate over their lot of living among teenagers who were quite profane to them. The Hansburys and the Carlins, also good neighbors, fared slightly better, as they had grown sons to stand up for them.

Strong prejudice against Jews and African-Americans existed then, and the one black family who moved in, across from us, were subjected to almost as much venom and as many racist graffiti on their doors and mailboxes as we were.

Another family with whom we got on well were the Hursts, a quiet Irish-American couple who lived across from us. Their daughter, Carol, and I would each pitch in a nickel, walk to the variety store across the Revere Beach Parkway, and buy a gigantic dill pickle. With great relish we took it home, divided it in half, and sat down on the steps of the incinerator in front of my house to savor it, amid the stench of burning garbage and the filth around us. It was a miracle that we didn't come down with dysentery or some other disease. That was our gossip corner, too.

While living there, my friends and I attended the Carter School, whose principal was Joseph Schultz. He was a tall, dark, attractive man of military bearing. When he had to substitute for our science teacher, he got even the most bored students' attention riveted, as he explained to us about molecular impact. Melvin Coburn's U.S. history classes were interesting and exciting, as he told us about the smuggling the original "patriots" did, and asked us how we would feel if we were in the place of the American Indians, being dispossessed of their lands and way of life by the white man. It was Mr. Coburn who first instilled in me a sense of obligation to Native Americans, to undo some of the harm that white people had done to them. I am very grateful to him for that. Notwithstanding his short stature, Mr. Coburn was a fiery, dynamic teacher. He took an interest in our personal problems, as well. Many of us have progressed in life because of his efforts.

Another dynamic teacher we had was Francis Mahoney, our algebra teacher. Tall, thin, with lively blue eyes, and dark brown hair with a cowlick arising from the top of his head, Mr. Mahoney had an unusually great capacity for explaining difficult problems. To cut through the dryness of the math, he put a good number of jokes into the problems, and kept our attention welded to the course. One of the brightest students in our class,

Rodney Masejewski, quite often ended up being the unwitting object of these jokes. In reference to Rodney's surname, Mr. Mahoney used to joke about a particular ship, calling out, "There she stands, Massachusetts." On another occasion Mr. Mahoney was referring to Noah Webster, who compiled the dictionary, and Rodney asked, "You mean the Noah who was in the boat?" To this Mr. Mahoney replied, "Sure, he was sailing around in a boat for forty days, and he couldn't think of anything else to do, so he wrote a dictionary," at which point we all burst out laughing.

As for other fine educators, Sumner Bloom, a bit stocky, dark-featured, and handsome, was our English teacher. He prepared us for future speaking careers, with the use of outlines and original material as the basis for our projects. He helped me immeasurably, as I used to dread oral presentations, with my knees knocking and stuttering in my speech. He got me relaxed enough to give a talk, and do it well. With all this wonderful educational background, unfortunately the Carter School burned to the ground in the 1970's, a great loss to the people of Chelsea. An apartment complex was later erected in its stead.

After graduating from Carter School, my classmates and I attended Chelsea High School, which became a melting pot for students from all over Chelsea. We had an excellent academic course to prepare us for college and careers. In our sophomore year we had tall, deep-voiced Mr. Shapiro for English, and he got us used to writing original theme compositions, as well as the usual required grammar. He was also very empathetic in helping students out with personal problems, with a fatherly warmth.

Aaron Kipnes's biology classes were "something else," to say the least. Barely five feet tall, with a balding head over piercing, dark eyes rimmed by glasses, Mr. Kipnes spoke with a deep, powerful voice that could be heard all the way down the corridor. He believed in being pragmatic in demonstrating to us, dissecting the formaldehyde-preserved bodies of snakes and octopi, as well as frogs and worms. Once he scared the daylights out of an unsuspecting girl by dangling from his forceps in front of her a preserved octopus. This seldom happened though, and if a student discreetly expressed a fear of reptiles to him, Mr. Kipnes took the time and patience after school to help the student get over the phobia. He always rewarded the student who tried hard with great praise, publicly.

Mrs. Maureen Kelly, our junior-year English teacher, was middle-aged, always dressed in a suit and blouse, with wavy, white hair falling to her shoulders. Like Aaron Kipnes, she was given to bursts of anger now and then, but considering how many students skipped homework assignments and gave stupid answers, I wonder that they managed to control their tempers at all. I benefited greatly from Mrs. Kelly's rigorous course in the Greek and English classics, her heavy emphasis on composition, and her insistence on promptness in completing assignments.

As for math courses, if you could make it through short, blond, attractive Mrs. Alice Sandberg's geometry classes, you could make it through college math courses.

Tall dark-featured, handsome Mr. Nathan Margolis, with a receding hairline and a very commanding manner, was our headmaster. He gave us excellent academic, as well as personal, guidance, in conjunction with our guidance counselor, Eli Richman, one of the most skilled and dedicated educators in the field. Between the two of them we all got the best preparation for college and vocational schools possible. Mr. Francis Mahoney, to whom I have already referred as our algebra teacher, later followed in Mr. Margolis's footsteps as Chelsea High School headmaster. We were very fortunate to have these sincere, dedicated people as our educators, to mention only a few. They set us in good stead for future endeavors.

In the meantime, many of the young people of our neighborhood worked their way through high school and partly through college. It made us proud of what we earned. I recall that some of us from the housing project even used to climb towering Powder Horn Hill to school just to save the nickel from carfare. In those days, of course, the cost of living was much less than it is now, and there was no inflation; the standard of living was better than the current one, with little homelessness. There was one family, whom we shall call the Stokers, who ultimately had eleven children, some of whom were very unruly, so that no one wanted them as tenants, and they could not afford a home of their own. I remember well several of the children who went to the Williams School with us. Much of the time they were in trouble of one sort or another. Ultimately, the Stokers left Chelsea for another community.

Lastly, with regard to the cost of living, our family got quite upset when the landlord raised the rent on our four-room apartment from twenty-six to forty dollars a month, back in 1955. That, I believe, was the beginning of the time of inflation. At first I worked as a maid, and managed to take myself off welfare. I scrubbed floors in a nursing home five to seven days a week, before I could get a job as a nurse's aide in a local hospital. Besides, I was under age, so I had to wait until I was sixteen before I could legitimately work. I enjoyed very much taking care of elderly people, and I kept one job for three years. That way I could save up for nursing school. At one point a girl named Bobby and I tried our hand at laundry work, and burned spots on some of the linens till we learned to iron better. Fortunately, the supervisor, a compassionate lady named Mary, overlooked our mistakes and gave us the benefit of the doubt as we improved.

Others of our schoolmates, including Sheldon Cohen, worked at selling the local newspaper, the *Chelsea Record.* Sheldon was very dear to his father and stepmother. She had just finished redecorating his bedroom, to surprise him when he returned from Vietnam. He telegrammed them that he would be home the next day. Sheldon became the first local boy to die in combat in the Vietnam War, the day before he was to return to America. Everyone in Chelsea was devastated when we heard the news of Sheldon's death. The Vietnam war was no longer some far-away conflict; it was now in our own community. Richard Brunelle, a pleasant fellow with whom I had gone through school, was among the more fortunate, and managed to return from the war alive.

There was another war that had to be fought during the 1950's, and that was the dreadful polio epidemic that hit the United States. I well recall our experience in the Boston area. We had a relative who lived in the Stratton Field housing project in Dorchester with her four children, and the disease spread like wildfire through the heavily congested apartments. A next-door neighbor would suddenly come down with polio, and before the third day had elapsed, would have expired. People feared to let their children play with other neighbors' children, keeping them carefully indoors. Many even feared to send their children to school, as the polio epidemic began to spread, without any warning, without any discrimination between the rich and the poor, the young and the elderly, or the strong and the weak. There was no way of escaping the invisible killer. The epidemic went on for many months, claiming thousands of lives, before abating.

During this time Dr. Jonas Salk and Dr. Albert Bruce Sabin, together with many other physicians and microbiologists, worked feverishly to discover and then treat the poliomyelitis virus. In the late 1950's Dr. Salk developed the vaccine to immunize against the polio virus, and then in 1959 Dr. Sabin perfected the trivalent oral polio drink, thus finally bringing the disease under control. Unfortunately, until the discovery of the vaccines thousands of people were left quadriplegic or hemiplegic, never to be able to use the lower parts of their bodies again, and in some cases to need total care for the rest of their lives. The polio epidemic had dealt a devastating blow to the entire American community before it was finally brought under control.

After the terrible polio epidemic subsided in the United States came a new social era. It was the beginning of rock and roll, with bands such as Bill Haley and the Comets singing and playing "Rock Around the Clock." This rock and roll fever remained in the country for another twelve years or so. It included other world-famous performers, such as the Beatles, for whom most girls of the day went "head over heels." However, by far the wildest reaction by young women was to the singing and guitar playing of Elvis Presley. With his aggressive, sexually provocative manner, as he sang "Don't Be Cruel," Elvis had thousands of young girls going into wild frenzies, rushing at him on the stage and throwing themselves at him, literally. He gave his security guards more than their share of work to do, at each performance. In the mid-sixties the craze over Presley started to die down.

Then big box office turnouts started to come for a brilliant player of brass instruments, Al Hirt. He played beautiful jazz music for hours on end, the perspiration rolling down his face, over a heavy-set build. I personally never cared for rock and roll music at all. However, though I was never that much of a jazz fan either, I really enjoyed Al Hirt's music in that it was true artistry. I wish I had some records of Al Hirt's music, so that I could enjoy playing them. My first stepfather, Gerald Siegel (my mother Ethel's second husband), of blessed memory, left me quite a collection of classical and Hebrew classical records, which I cherish.

We had a wonderful father-daughter relationship, which I shall soon describe.

As for the fad crazes that took place in the fifties and sixties, one was the dress fashion called the *saque de Paris*. The *saque* was really nothing more than an over-inflated dress that was gathered at the neck and the ankles, with no real style to it. Nevertheless, it was in vogue for a time, so many women flocked to buy several of these garments. However, one fashion that came into the forefront during that time and took much dignity away from women was the mini-skirt, which sometimes came to above mid-thigh level. Teen-agers and even women in their twenties and thirties began buying mini-skirts by the thousands. The only rationale I can see to this occurrence was that it took place during the "sexy sixties." Even many of the nurses with whom I worked in Boston began wearing mini-skirt uniforms, much to the distress of myself and many of the nursing supervisors.

My own way of rebelling against the mini-skirt was to wear longer skirts and dresses, and to occasionally wear Indian *chorli* blouses with *sarees*. This was to let people know that ultra-long was more beautiful and more respectable than ultra-short. The calf-length skirt and dress have come more into fashion lately.

I believe that one of the most unfortunate consequences of the mini-skirt, together with American parents allowing sexual permissiveness among their children, was that it led to high-school premarital sex. This was followed, of course, by unwanted pregnancies. Children having children is not a rational idea. It has unfortunately continued through the current era, accompanied by widespread battering of wives, girlfriends, and children.

As for my teenage years, I was totally accepted by my first stepfather, Gerald Siegel, a blind man, when I was thirteen years old. As I mentioned earlier, Ethel and Izzy had divorced when I was four years old, but to this day I can recall the abuse that I suffered during their marriage. Although it is not easy for anyone, especially a blind person, to accept as his own child a confused thirteen-year-old, as most teenagers are in this society, Gerry (whom I called Pa) gave me so much love and understanding, as well as discipline. He never lifted a hand to me; he only had to give me one stern look and I would realize that I had done something wrong. Pa was a fairly attractive man, five feet nine inches tall, with a good build, a squarish face, a slightly long nose, and full lips. He was bald, save for grayish black hair at the sides and back of his head. He had black eyebrows above dark brown eyes.

Pa had a fantastic sense of humor and could make a joke out of the worst situations, making life in general more tolerable. As we walked arm-in-arm down the street with his seeing-eye German Shepherd, Julie, Pa always introduced me as his daughter, and I was in seventh heaven.

My first stepfather, Gerald Siegel.

He was also very perceptive, and notwithstanding his blindness, could tell me if someone was cheating at a card game. His sensitivity was unmatched.

Pa bought me one of the finest Smith-Corona typewriters when the time came for me to enter college in 1960. Even though he was blind, Pa manually examined one typewriter after another in the store, ignoring price, until he was satisfied that this particular typewriter was the best choice for me. It served me well through two years of college and three years of nursing school. It was one of my most cherished possessions, besides my family pictures and the monogrammed ring with a diamond in it that Pa had left me. The typewriter is an important part of Pa's legacy to Dalya and me, and we must always keep it in the family. I only got to spend a precious five years with this wonderful man before he died of complications of diabetes mellitus.

Gerry himself had been orphaned shortly after his Bar Mitzvah, his mother, a widow whose picture I still have, having died of the same disease that ultimately killed him. They had been members of the Lithuanian Jewish community. We must keep in mind that sixty years ago there were not half the medical advances there are now, so that many more people died of diabetes than do now. Thus Pa, his sister Mildred, and his brother George became foster children. It was a life filled with hardships, as Gerry lost his sight in his late twenties, and many a landlady robbed him of money, jewelry, and other belongings when he lived in rooming houses. His first wife left him as he became blind, a fact for which I will never forgive her, though she and I have not met.

Despite these hardships, Gerry never displayed bitterness toward me or anyone else around him (except occasionally Ethel, who with her mental vagaries could be very irritating). Pa always helped teach me how to reason out problems dispassionately, examining all the relevant factors before making a judgment. It is true that those who have the least often give the most.

I think I shall never forgive myself for taking a final exam when Gerry was dying. I assumed that I would dash right home from college, and then go directly to the hospital. I should have postponed the exam and been at his bedside instead. I was later told by the nurses that Pa's last words were a wish that I had done well in my finals. Not until ten years after his death did I become aware of the great love I had had in this very kind, selfless man.

Through participation in Gerry's and Mama Tzipah's organizations, I was introduced to one of the finest humanitarians, the late Father Thomas Carroll, founder of the Catholic Center for All the Blind, which later was named for him as the Carroll Center for the Blind. The motto under that title read, "We consider need, not race or creed." Father Carroll lived that motto his whole life, before the birth of the civil rights movements of the 1960's. He gave help to any blind person or family who may have had an additional problem, such as deafness, needing a hearing aid, or finances, needing a grocery order, or special household appliances for the blind, without caring about their ethnic backgrounds.

Neither did he include proselytizing in any way during ecumenical or interfaith activities. Father Carroll always bestowed Chanukah greetings on his Jewish clients at combined Christmas-Chanukah parties (which were held annually), as well as bestowing Christmas blessings on the Christian members. At his stately height near six feet, with dark eyes and glasses, gray hair, and a rather somber manner about him, as he steadied himself with his cane Father Carroll was the epitome of humility. Now and then there would be a twinkle in his eye, especially when he encountered someone who needed a morale booster. A young atheist at the Center once said to Father Carroll, "You'll have to forgive me, Father, but I don't believe in your G-d," to which Father Carroll replied, "That's all right. God bless you, my son." I was deeply touched by that, as I was by the rest of Father Carroll's way of dealing with people and sharing love. It was a privilege for me to do volunteer work for him. In addition to the late Anne Sullivan, Helen Keller, and the Perkins family, to name a few, Father Carroll probably did more than anyone else in his generation for the betterment of all blind people.

Father Carroll's book, *Blindness,*[1] though it was not on the best-seller list, is one of the most deeply sensitive and informative books I have ever read. In it he dispelled many myths about blindness, such as the idea that blind people have much more highly developed hearing and smell, to compensate for their blindness. Some blind people learn to make more use of these senses to help them function, but they are not more highly developed than others. Also, he carefully explained that none of the rest of us would like it if someone suddenly came up from behind and grabbed us to deter us from a harmful object; and thus neither does a blind person appreciate this. One has only to call to a blind person from behind to alert him or her to the danger.

Things that most of us who are sighted take for granted, such as a woman's making up her face, are a considerable challenge for a blind person who does not want an uncomplimentary blob of makeup on one side of her face, with little or none on the other side. Blind people also attach great importance to having their garments attractively matched, making it necessary to arrange their clothes in a carefully designed closet and drawer sequence. In addition, Father Carroll stressed the blind person's need for professional esteem, to be able to feel fulfillment in acquiring and keeping a suitable job.

Furthermore, among important pointers stressed in Father Carroll's book was locomotion. Sighted people who want to help lead a blind person (if the blind person so chooses) should offer their arm to the blind person to hold onto. This is preferable to taking hold of the blind person's arm and pushing him or her forward. This is most disconcerting and irritating for a person who doesn't know what he or she is stepping onto or into. Sighted people should always keep that in mind.

Father Carroll's book, *Blindness,* taught me something equally valuable, if not more valuable: that no one should ever take anyone or anything for granted. Our senses should not be taken for granted; neither should people, or their abilities or their attitudes, be taken for granted. The whole world runs interdependently, whether we think so or not. Sometimes it's better to ask, when in doubt. So far as I am concerned, this book is a classic that should be made required reading in all academic courses in high schools throughout the United States.

FOUR

COLLEGE, NURSING SCHOOL, AND PUBLIC HEALTH

As I mentioned earlier, it was while I was in my sophomore year at Boston State College that Pa took ill and died, while simultaneously Mama Tzipah got cancer of the ribs and had to be operated on at another hospital. With all these things combined, plus financial problems, I left college at the end of the first semester of the second year.

For the next seven months I worked steadily as a nurse's aide at the Revere Memorial, where I had worked part-time for the previous two years. Together with a salary, this gave me the time I badly needed for reflection on life in general, and a rest from mental exhaustion. It was the first really good break I had had at a job, and I am indebted to the late Mrs. Leone E. Taylor, then the Director of Nurses, for her guidance and consideration. She was an "old school" nurse, and believed in promptness, respect for authority, and hard work. Also, she believed in giving credit to those who tried hard at the job, which I did, though I was very slow at first. She gave me the opportunity to catch up, and taught me everything she could about nursing.

In September 1962 I entered the Whidden Memorial Hospital School of Nursing, where I ultimately completed an excellent three-year program of study. It was intensive education, with not much time left for fooling around, and we got a thorough grounding in each of the fields of nursing, including medical-surgical, pediatrics, obstetrics, and disaster nursing. What we did not get, because these courses are not commonly taught in the United States, were nurse-midwifery and inoculations. Our instructors, including Ivy O'Donnell, Joan Pizzano, Edna Gerry, Gwendolyn Lawson (our former Director), and Dorothy Ching, to name a few, were supportive, and our Director, Dolores Hernandez, did much to update the program.

Among the doctors who taught us, I distinctly remember Dr. John B. Williams in medical-surgical, and Dr. H. Arthur Berson in pediatrics, who had also saved my life when I was a child. They both emphasized the importance of carefully noting every symptom the patient exhibited, including symptoms the patients were afraid to tell us about, such as rectal bleeding. One man bled all over the toilet, but feared to tell us. A cleaning lady observed the bleeding, reported it to a student nurse, and she in turn reported it to the surgeon. The patient was then operated on for cancer of the recto-sigmoid colon, which ultimately saved his life.

Dr. Berson also stressed the importance of our picking up on symptoms in small children, who often couldn't adequately express what it was that bothered them. For example, noting a child's squatting or simply lying down on the floor, together with pale or bluish coloration, probably indicated open heart disease. Dr. Williams was ultra-conservative, often keeping post-surgical patients in the hospital an extra couple of days, to make sure there would not be any complications, such as blood clots or infection. Both physicians stressed our using good, common sense in caring for patients. They also impressed upon us the importance of empathy, for no patient complaint is to be ignored.

Dr. Williams was also very generous, treating all of us in our junior year to a formal evening out for dinner and cocktails at one of Boston's finest nightclubs. We all dressed in floor-length gowns or fancy dresses, and all of us lined up afterwards to give Dr. Williams a kiss of thanks. He was in his seventies at the time, with Dr. Berson being in his forties then. I'm sure that none of us forgot their teachings or their caring.

I will always be indebted to my classmate, Peggy Bellefontaine Bailey, for her having shown me all of the techniques necessary when working on the night shift, as I was a slow learner. Peggy never condescended to me in any way, but in her own kind manner showed me the ins and outs of doing charge work on the night shift, to which I had hitherto not been exposed very much. She was a "true blue" friend. I also owe a debt of gratitude to an older nurse who worked at the Whidden, and that was Flossy Isaacs, who showed me the techniques in intensive care nursing. This involved a young girl who suffered a severe toxic reaction during anesthesia. Flossy went over the vital signs and neurological signs monitoring, physical therapy, and total patient care necessary for this patient. Flossy prepared me very adequately for the critical care work I was later to have thrust upon me.

Notwithstanding the intensive education at nursing school, we did have some social life. Three other classmates, Diane Mutty, Martha Lindsey, and my roommate, Joanne Lucien, and I teamed up not only for studying together, but also for good times. We were all invited to sleep over at the Lucien's home one time, where we got the warmest hospitality. Mrs. Lucien, a widow, made us all feel completely at home and shared everything freely with us.

Though the four of us were brought up to respect authority and follow the rules, temptation got into us, and one night we decided to walk down the hill to a beer parlor in Everett Square, where they served excellent roast beef sandwiches for very reasonable prices. That was not the worst infraction though. We decided to wear long coats over full student nurse uniforms, just to prove that we could break the rules and get away with it, which we did. (Off nursing school grounds only street clothes were allowed to be worn.) It wasn't a big deal, but we all got such a bang out of the event, including eating out at a liquor place. We just ordered Coke with our sandwiches, which were very thick and delicious, and got a charge out of eating out among many men who were consuming alcoholic beverages. We managed to sneak back to the dormitory undetected afterwards.

However, the real hell-raising at nursing school took place at the freshman initiations. First of all, the upper class students to whom we "little sisters" were given had designed hilarious hats made completely out of balloons, which we were supposed to wear all day, even to our classes. Everyone, including our instructors, broke up laughing. Then came the real shebang that night in the nursing school auditorium. All the freshman were dressed in sporty, makeshift costumes, and were to be punished for any wrong answer to an upper class student. A fellow classmate, Patty Hanaford, got squirted in the face twice with a water gun when she gave wrong answers to a junior student, and I got hit in the face twice with cream pies for talking back to a junior student. One of our instructors, Ivy O'Donnell, had a poodle, Fru Fru, which set about promptly licking off my face each time I sat down. Others of us had to run around in circles several times for wrong answers. All in all, our initiation was very much a fun night.

However, our class, when we became juniors, were much less thoughtful when it came time for us to initiate the new freshmen. One of my fellow classmates, Dina Freedman, who had an especially mischievous inclination, thought up the idea for a new student named Edith, who had a morbid fear of worms: to make Edith walk blindfolded through a couple of bedpans filled with spaghetti and tomato sauce. Edith did so on command, but screamed her lungs out in the process, as Dina chimed in, "Well, what does it feel like you're walking through?" A few moments later, as her blindfold was removed, Edith was much relieved to see it was only spaghetti. A few others of us got the idea of taking the skeleton that we used for our anatomy and physiology classes, gingerly carrying it up the stairs to the second floor bathroom, and seating it on the toilet. One of the freshmen girls opened the toilet door and let out a shriek as she saw the guiltless skeleton sitting on the hopper. Another classmate grabbed her before she fell to the floor. We also had a variety of castigations, such as squirting with water guns, as had been done to us during initiation. Some less severe initiation jokes included hanging different colored sheets of toilet paper as curtains on the outsides of freshman dorm rooms. I thought that was rather cute, plus you could always use the toilet paper afterwards.

The school play, under the leadership of one of our instructors, Joan Delory, was probably the funniest climax event of our three years at Whidden. Several of our fellow classmates were born naturals as actresses in the skits. The most hilarious skit by far was the one where we used a garden hose and bucket to make believe we were giving an enema to a patient. Donna O'Connell played the patient, while another student, given the name of Mrs. Pizzonnell (combining Miss Pizzano's and Mrs. O'Donnell's names), portrayed the fastidious instructor, who kept shouting to the two "students" giving the enema, "Now watch your body mechanics, girls. Watch your body mechanics." While this went on, Gilda Romanelli, who absolutely broke everyone in the audience into peals of laughter, portrayed the hospital cleaning woman, wearing a drab housedress and a kerchief tied over her hair. Gill busily went about mopping the area, including the patient's rear end, as water gushed out of the hose, and the "patient" screamed, "I can't hold it. It's coming out." Gill kept a dead serious face throughout the skit, and jutting her rear end out to mop under the bed, kept on steadfastly mopping. I don't recall Phyllis Diller or the late Lucille Ball as ever having been funnier than Gill.

In addition, during the school play, we had a skit in which twelve of us were chosen to represent the months of the year. Peggy Bellefontaine (soon to become Peggy Bailey) portrayed the January New Year baby, wearing a gigantic "diaper" with a deliberate smear of brown on the backside of it. How they came to choose the most observant Jew in the nursing school to play Saint Patrick for the month of March I am not quite sure, but I was chosen to play that role. When given the signal, I marched onto the center of the stage, wearing a short-sleeved green blouse, a long green skirt, and a huge four-leaf clover pin on my blouse, as I swung a *shelaylie* in my right hand. A burst of laughter and applause greeted me, as most people in the audience knew I was Jewish, while the background record played "MacNamara's Band."

Last but not least came the crowning event we had all waited for, the senior prom. However, getting us to the prom was something else. My roommate, Joanne, and I needed dates for the prom, so Mama got a bright idea and said, "I know what. I'll give a tea party and invite Charlie from upstairs to introduce him to Joanne." It seemed a bit far-fetched, but Charlie was a decent fellow with a pleasant personality, and the party came off well, with Joanne and Charlie getting along fine, and agreeing to go to the prom together. My date was a fellow named Marty, whom I'd met through the Young Adults at the Jewish Community Center. Joanne and

I set out looking for suitable gowns at second-hand shops. The dresses we found actually looked quite lovely on us, with our hair done up, wearing high heels, earrings, and other matching accessories.

All in all, the prom went off fairly well, with Dianne, Martha, Joanne, and me (as well as the rest of our fellow classmates) and our dates dancing, then sitting together at a table in the reception-dance hall having a good time. We all took color photos of the occasion, of course, as remembrances. As I look back on it now, I miss those relatively carefree days of fun that the four of us girls used to have together. I would very much like the four of us to be able to get together again, to see who got married, how many children we had, where we lived, and what experiences we had lived through since last we saw each other. The years pass us by too quickly—for me, anyway.

I regret very much, as many others do, that some years ago the Whidden Memorial Hospital School of Nursing was permanently closed, in order to create only baccalaureate nursing programs, to put nursing more on a par with other professions, such as accounting and engineering. The excellence of the clinical and theoretical aspects of the three-year, hospital-based, diploma nursing schools can never be fully replaced. In a crisis situation, it is far more helpful to have a good clinical nurse than a college-trained administrator caring for acutely ill patients. Our nursing school, the Whidden Memorial, served the community well in that purpose.

Our junior year at the Whidden was indelibly marked by an event of unbelievable horror and tragedy that we shared with all other Americans: the assassination of President John F. Kennedy. I recall distinctly that five of us were laid up in the Danvers Infirmary, our psychiatric affiliation for three months, with ptomaine poisoning from some hot cakes we had eaten. (The food was often bad there; G-d help the poor patients who had to eat it constantly.) As we lay doubled up with abdominal pain, our housemother suddenly burst into the Infirmary to say that the President had been assassinated. We were all shocked and in disbelief, as were so many others. Suddenly the abdominal pain didn't seem to matter anymore. We tried to rally ourselves, but I began to cry uncontrollably, as I believe several million other Americans were doing.

By that evening we had gotten over the ptomaine, and we all tried to find a way to cope with our grief. This took place as we were coincidentally packing up to leave our psychiatric affiliation and return to school. Upon my return, for the first time in my life I wasted food, as I got up from lunch, all choked up from watching the President's funeral on the television set up in the hospital dining room. From there I headed for surgery, cried my eyes out in the locker room, and then proceeded to scrub for the surgeon. It was a day of tragedy for all of us, as President Kennedy's young, vigorous life was snuffed out like a match.

My classmates and I graduated June 30, 1965, and I completed the course with distinction, as did my two good friends, Martha and Dianne, to bring honor to our families. I am indebted to the education we received at the Whidden, as among others, the disaster nursing course stood me in good stead when I became a triage nurse in the Yom Kippur War in 1973, which I will describe later.

It was while I was in college and nursing school that I began to see more strongly the meaning of bigotry. Whenever the president of our college addressed the student body, he began by making the sign of the Cross over everyone. In nursing school, as we entered the main lounge, there was a picture of what was supposed to be Jesus hanging on the wall. The likeness was absurd in that they showed him as fair-skinned, with blue eyes and light brown hair. Jesus was a Semite (whose exact likeness no one knows), most likely a medium-brown-skinned, brown-eyed man with black, wavy hair. Both of these institutions, by the way, were supposed to be nonsectarian.

As for the rest of my college work, the two subjects that I liked best were French and biology. I was not yet mature enough to digest Dante's *Inferno* or the course in physical science, and to do well at them. I had intended to get a bachelor's degree in biology, but had done poorly in genetics, and had never completed enough courses for that degree.

After nursing school came a year of public health nursing in Boston, and that was when my linguistic abilities came in handy. I discovered myself to be the only Spanish-speaking nurse in a community of three thousand Spanish-speaking patients. My patients, many of whom were quite poor, were very warm to me, as I came by for new baby visits. They would often insist that I join them for enchiladas and tea before leaving the house. I was also able to teach medication, nutrition, and isolation techniques to tuberculosis patients and new mothers in Spanish, as well as teaching the English-speaking patients. The work was extremely rewarding, and I also became educated as to the meaning of poverty, unwed mothers, and oppression of the poor by the rich.

I began to see where the seeds of racial hatred are sown when I visited apartments in Boston's South End, most of which were inhabited by African-Americans and Hispanics who were forced to pay high rents to absentee landlords who hardly heated the apartments in winter. In some cases, the railings and staircases literally crumbled as I ascended the stairs. Hundreds of cockroaches fell from the walls and ceilings as I entered the apartments. On several occasions babies had been bitten by rats. The department of housing inspection did not enforce extermination of roaches and rodents. Many small children came down with repeated bouts of streptococcus throat infections and pneumonias, obviously linked to the freezing conditions in the apartments in winter. This occurred even though the parents did their best to keep the children bundled up snugly. The building code of Boston required that buildings with more than four stories had to have elevators, but this rule was seldom enforced. It was a special hardship for many elderly people and those with heart conditions to have to clamber up six flights of stairs.

As I walked up West Newton, West Dedham, and Tremont Streets in the South End, I began to understand why many downtrodden people living in this area could develop a hatred for the "white establishment" (landlords and government). They could see, a short distance away, the luxury of the Prudential Tower and opulent local hotels for the very wealthy, while they had nothing. I could understand the hatred of parents whose child's death certificate I had just received cited pneumonia as the cause of death—while their wealthy landlords dined on sirloin steak at the Top of the Hub Restaurant, with a fine cordial drink. I started to feel guilty as I bought a five-dollar ticket to enjoy with a friend an exhibit at the Museum of Fine Arts, followed by dinner at the Kon-Tiki Ports restaurant, while my patients could barely afford to eat meat. While my cousin and I enjoyed a Stravinsky concert at Boston's Symphony Hall for ten dollars a ticket, most of my patients could not even afford a ticket to the early matinee at a movie house. A college professor friend of mine decided that it was time that they had a third car in the family for his son (at a cost of four thousand dollars), while the people of the *barrio* (poverty-stricken, ghetto area) walked to and from work because they did not have enough money for carfare. The walk was often a half hour each way, and often very dangerous for a man or a woman to be traversing alone, especially after dark. In winter I began to empathize more with my patients, as I left the well-shoveled sidewalks of my neighborhood to slide and almost break my neck (with heavy, ripple-soled boots on), going on house calls on West Canton Street, where the landlords had not cleared the sidewalks off or even sanded them.

A few young prostitutes who lived in my district always greeted me, and I returned the greetings. G-d only knows, if each of these girls had had a parent at home, or even a caring friend to whom they could turn for love and advice, they might not have followed this path in life. In those days it was common courtesy for neighbors in the district, including prostitutes and drug addicts, to greet public health nurses and be greeted in return. Our business was simply health care for residents of our districts, and matters of law were left to the police. Thus the local lawbreakers rarely bothered us nurses, as long as our hats and badges were in full view to identify us. On occasion some thugs might hassle us, but as a rule it was nothing serious. Quite often we were befriended by people we had cared for in the district, and they protected us. One day I was walking down Dartmouth Street with a fellow public health nurse, when two men whistled at us. I turned around and said, "Thank you," to which the men turned around, surprised, and replied, "You're welcome."

However, there was much more to tell of the needless suffering of humanity. It was to be found in caring for active tuberculosis cases and unwed mothers, all too many of whom abounded in the barrio in Boston's South End in 1966. As I came to know these people individually, I found most of them to have been abused and deprived by both family and society. One such situation I came upon was in seeking out an alcoholic named Danny who had infected many children in his family with tuberculosis. One of my "grapevine" people directed me to a certain saloon on Tremont Street, not far from the old National Theatre. I did not find him there, but was immediately offered ginger ale, gratis, which I accepted. Soon I learned in what house on Tremont Street I could find the man I sought.

After climbing up four flights of dim, dirty stairs, I found this man in an apartment whose door was open, lying with three other inebriated men on a urine-soaked double mattress. Keeping a proper distance, I tried to communicate with Danny, telling him how important it was for him to come to the TB (tuberculosis) clinic regularly, for us to check him and make sure he had enough medication. I saw no point in telling him about the children he had infected at this point, thinking it better to discuss that with him when he was sober in the clinic. Amazingly enough, he did respond, and came to the clinic a week later. There we were able to counsel him about the importance of staying away from the relatives' children until he was doing much better. We knew that he would ultimately go into and out of alcoholic episodes, but at least we had a handle on the situation.

Danny had come East from a poverty situation, hoping to better himself, only to discover racial rejection. With one rejection after another, and money running out, he turned in depression to panhandling and alcohol. As I got to know Danny better, I saw that he was not a hard-core degenerate. A program of vocational education, coupled with jobs for the needy, would have done wonders for him.

Turning to the unwed mothers that we ministered to, I found out quickly that most of them were not tramps, but rather girls who had had little, if any, parental guidance. They often came from alcoholic and/or battered wife and child home situations, with hardly a soul to turn to for love and nurturing. Many of them were consumed by guilt feelings about having brought an unwanted child into the world, the result of a brief, mostly physical relationship with a man whom the girl thought would love her. Then the man would abandon her as soon as he found out she was pregnant, often leaving her without anyone to take her in and comfort her. These women were close-mouthed, withdrawn, and sometimes hostile. Though at first I found it difficult to cope with these situations, slowly I learned to care for these young women. I listened to their problems and offered liaison services, such as social service and emergency grocery orders. This would be done through either the local welfare office or church groups. After all, why should the children be made to suffer for acts they had not brought on themselves, and understood less?

One young African-American woman, aged seventeen, had come up North from Virginia, thinking that the grass would be greener up here. Then she discovered that the young man who had gotten her pregnant had walked out on her. She was polite and open to suggestions as to how to care for her baby son, but she was steeped in some very backward ideas she had inherited from her mother. I was aghast when I saw Emma taking the baby's urine-soaked diaper and rubbing the baby's face with it, as she said her mother had taught her. However, I slowly suggested the idea of washing the child with an inexpensive baby shampoo and water, and then applying Vaseline or lanolin between the child's legs to prevent diaper rash. (Desitin was too expensive a salve for Emma to buy.)

What one does not do is tell a mother that her own mother's ideas were wrong or dirty; rather, one tries substitution. In this case it worked, as this young mother was sincerely interested in her child's well-being. I also told Emma that she could get, free of charge, vitamin A and D supplements, as well as immunizations for the baby and referrals for social service help, when she came to our well-baby clinic. She came a couple of weeks later, in good faith, and promptly received proper attention for her son, including the items I just mentioned. However, their living accommodations were dreadful, with badly peeling and cracking lead paint, hordes of cockroaches, dimly lit staircases, and broken locks on the entrance doors of the buildings.

There is a shortage of suitable, affordable housing in Boston today; forty years ago that shortage was far worse. Often a number of families would "shack up" in one apartment just to be able to exist. These circumstances somewhat resembled those in modern-day Appalachia. Thank heavens that we have had a local organization called Massachusetts Tenants Organization, which has made remarkable strides on behalf of indigent, elderly, and handicapped tenants, as well as for tenants in general. We still have a long way to go, though, before equitable rents are legally established, together with condominium conversion control.

There was another heart-rending situation I came upon in my district, and that was of a young boy who had been born both blind and mentally deficient. He was being cared for with much dedication by his widowed father, a working man, and the father's elderly mother, who constantly washed, fed, and changed the child. Thanks to the intervention of Mrs.

Hayes, my second supervisor in the district, the child was institutionalized in a home for the blind, where he could receive good care. This also relieved this beautiful Hispanic family of the terrible strain they had endured for five years.

The last appalling situation that must be told about here is that of the family of a mentally retarded Caucasian woman who got together with a different man every year and produced another child almost yearly. There were nine children, the oldest being thirteen years old and more or less the caretaker, with the rest of the children going down the age range to eight months old. It was plain to see that the thirteen-year-old boy, given the opportunity, could have been of good intellect. However, the pathos of the situation was that he had no escape from this household to be able to better himself.

As the other nurse and I entered the house, we found it reeking of urine and feces. The one double bed and the couch were saturated with urine, and dirty diapers were strewn about the floor. As the older boy noticed each of the younger siblings getting wet, he picked them up out of the wet area and set them down somewhere else. He cradled in his arms the youngest one, who was crying, with a look of sadness on his face. When we opened the refrigerator, we found a carton of sour milk, packages of rancid cheese and butter, a loaf of moldy bread, plus some rotted fruit.

In those days the Division of Child Guardianship was not as active as it is now, and people did not have half the awareness they have now about Battered Child Syndrome. I was told by a colleague of mine, "You can't tell people what to do with their bodies," referring to the concept of enforced birth control. In pathetic cases such as this one, I believe society has an obligation to protect unwanted, neglected, and often abused children from incompetent parents. At least, in a country such as the People's Republic of China, if that retarded woman had conceived, she would have been required to have medically supervised abortions.

Society's first responsibility must be to the child, and to the Rights of the Child, if I may quote the late Dr. Henryk Goldshmidt, Father of the War Orphans. Every child should be loved, disciplined, and educated. Though the United States is not as progressive about birth control as China, at least there are the alternatives of adoptive homes, where deserving childless couples can hardly wait to nurture a homeless child. I cannot forget the feeling of frustration and sadness I had, as we left that house, having made our assessments, which would be passed in to headquarters. It was because of all these situations that I had to deal with as a public health nurse that I came to understand the well-known prayer, "G-d grant me the serenity to accept things I cannot change, courage to change the things I can, and wisdom to know the difference between the two."

On the positive side, one unique educational event happened while I was a district nurse in the South End in the company of the supervisor I already mentioned, Lillie Hayes. She took me with her to the Museum of Afro-American History, to hear the great American poet, the late Langston Hughes, recite from his own poetry. I value this as having been one of the great educational opportunities of my life, and I am grateful to Lillie.

There was another positive event I experienced with the Hispanic community. Boston's Children's Hospital suddenly reported two cases (almost positive) of diphtheria in the South End. Hundreds of Hispanic families had not yet been inoculated against diphtheria and other diseases. Dr. William Duserick immediately set up a map with me for us to canvas West Newton Street, West Canton Street, West Dedham Street, and Tremont Street, with the list of necessary charts in our briefcases. The next day we set out, visiting tenement after tenement, and family after family, with me interpreting for Dr. Duserick his message of the urgent need for the parents to bring all of their children two days later, on Friday, to the South End Health Unit to be inoculated. They responded that if Senorita Zohar was there, they would come. However, if Senorita Zohar was not there, they would not come. (Zohar was my maiden name.) I promised them all that I would be there.

On Thursday other public health nurses and I set up a number of tables with trays of diphtheria/pertussis/tetanus, trivalent oral polio, measles/mumps/rubella, and smallpox inoculation vials, needles, syringes, and alcohol swabs in preparation for the patients expected to come on Friday. True to their word, the Hispanic parents came with all their children, the first three families arriving at 10:00 a.m. From that time till twelve noon twenty-five more families arrived, so that we had to send to headquarters for more inoculation materials. By three o'clock another fifty-odd families had come—and an outbreak of diphtheria, among other diseases, had been avoided. Dr. Frederick Maloof, one of the senior physicians, told me, "You know, Miss Zohar, Bill Duserick thinks the world of you, with your having gotten the whole Hispanic community inoculated." By five o'clock the rest of the families had been inoculated. Never in my life did I so much enjoy skipping coffee break and lunch break; it was for a good cause, which I will never forget.

To return to the subject of housing, much compact, modern housing has been erected in the South End to replace some of the dilapidated buildings that were torn down. However, there is still a sense of hopelessness among some of the decent, poor families who have to live in the crime-ridden Cathedral Housing project on Washington Street. There remains the bitterness and hostility of those who have no job and often no skills that are marketable. Their only outlet is to take drugs, to make them forget. These people project their problems onto unsuspecting others, and the result is a crime wave. Most of these people could be taught a trade, if given the opportunity. It has already been proven through the Cardinal Cushing Spanish Center, the Salvation Army, and other outreach agencies.

All in all, my year as a public health nurse in Boston's South End was one of the most enlightening experiences of my life.

After that came illness (later diagnosed as lactose intolerance), which interrupted my work. While I was hospitalized, a fellow patient, Noreen, and I struck up a conversation on the sunporch of Saint Elizabeth's Hospital. We decided to keep in touch after we left the hospital. That was how Noreen and I became best friends. Back in 1966, when Noreen and I were still single, we had a blast of a time together. Aside from going on shopping sprees and eating out now and then, we occasionally went to the City Club on a Saturday night, and there we had the most fun. Neither of us will ever forget the time I ended up with a date named Jack Kennedy and Noreen ended up with a date named Levite (which happens to be my tribe of descent from the twelve tribes of Israel). As Noreen and I came off the dance floor, we introduced our new dates to each other. We all burst out laughing, and Noreen said, "I knew it—you'd end up with an Irishman and I'd end up with a Jew!" The four of us went out for a snack at a restaurant in Kenmore Square after we left the City Club, before we all went home.

Noreen learned about Jewish culture from me, and she introduced me to her native Irish culture by attending events at the Eire Society with another friend named Maizie. Noreen's sister, Margaret, joined us on some of these occasions, and we all enjoyed the concerts and other events we attended. Since then, Noreen and I each married men of our own people, but we never lost contact with each other. On every Chanukah and Christmas since then, Noreen and Bill, her husband, and I exchange greetings and/or gifts. If I had my own sister to choose, I would have chosen Noreen. Whenever one of us has been in time of great need, we've always come through for each other, often more so than our families. Though Noreen now lives in Ireland, and I live in Boston, our sisterly bond will be kept for as long as we live.

After Noreen and I met, I did a few years of private duty nursing, which fitted in nicely with my taking some college courses toward a prospective college degree. Also in this line of work, I came to learn about some of the most complicated diseases in the world, including hemorrhagic diseases. In addition, as a private duty nurse, I got to know some of the most interesting people, some of them from the intelligentsia, and others who felt they could buy or sell people.

During that time I also came to work under the leadership of Dr. Charles Trey, one of the world's leading liver disease specialists—and an extremely dedicated man. We worked on some of Dr. Trey's critically ill patients, sometimes for sixteen hours at a stretch, with Dr. Trey remaining at the patient's side constantly. When we talk about Jews in America who give of themselves for the betterment of the Jewish community, we talk about the late Dr. Charles and Sonia Trey. Their contributions have included Project Rofeh (started under the aegis of Grand Rabbi Levi Horowitz of the Beth Pinchas Orthodox congregation), which helps Jews from around the world who have serious medical problems by providing medical care, room and board, and translation services here in the Boston area.

FIVE

LEARNING ABOUT NATIVE AMERICANS

THOSE CHILDHOOD YEARS BRING BACK OTHER MEMORIES TOO, MEMORIES OF THE SUFFERING OF A NAVAHO GIRLFRIEND I KNEW WHEN I WAS EIGHT YEARS OLD. Jean-Rose was two years younger than I. Her mother was Navaho and her father was an American of Anglo-Saxon descent. The beginning of her life was very sad, as her mother died giving birth to her, under atrocious reservation conditions. From what Jean-Rose's father, George, as well as my Native American friends, told me, the medical facilities had such poor equipment and drugs that they were a disgrace. When they took over the land by force, the Europeans, more commonly referred to as the White Men, promised the Native Americans, or Red Men, land with fresh-flowing water and plenty of green grass. Then they forced the Native Americans onto reservations with neither of the two.

To get back to Jean-Rose's and my friendship, whenever my Uncle Saul, who was her father's friend, brought her to our house, she and I enjoyed bicycling on our city block. On one occasion, when Jean-Rose was bicycling near her home, she caught her toe in her bicycle, and the toe had to be amputated. She had a very good spirit and recovered very well though.

Jean-Rose was raised mainly by her paternal grandmother, who was very kind to her. However, after the grandmother's death, when Jean-Rose was about eleven, her father remarried, this time to a white woman in her late teens, and they started raising a family immediately. It was ultimately a large family (of about ten children), and when Jean-Rose's father suddenly died in his early forties, Jean-Rose was left to feel very isolated and alone. Though I believe it was not the deliberate intention of Phyllis (her step-mother) to do so, Jean-Rose was excluded from the family mainstream, and as soon as she was old enough, she left Phyllis's home to set out on her own in life. About thirty years ago, she and I last saw each other and had lunch in Boston. Jean-Rose had married a white man (of much less refined calibre than she); they had conceived, and she had had a miscarriage to add to her miseries. We lost contact after that, very regrettably, and I would very much want to see Jean-Rose again before the end of our days.

It was far more tragic than that though. That an unusually bright, gifted young lady like Jean-Rose should have been denied the opportunity for a good educational future solely because she was a Native American was an ignominy. Jean-Rose was exceptionally attractive and could have been a fine model for Eileen Ford. She stood five feet five inches tall, with medium brown skin. She had arched, fine eyebrows set over beautiful dark brown eyes with long lashes, a small, straight nose, slightly elevated cheekbones, and fine, perfectly formed lips. Jean-Rose also had long, straight black hair and a fine figure. She had a natural warmth that glowed through her smile.

Through my experience with Jean-Rose, I came to be affiliated in adult life, as a volunteer, with the North American Indian Center of Boston, Inc. There I have helped to get needy Native American families furniture, clothing, and food from time to time. Through that organization I have come to know a number of fine people of the Wampanoag, Sioux, Micmac, Penobscot, and other tribes, and to learn about their cultures. The hand-made moccasins, earrings, and necklaces that my daughter and I possess are treasures to us. Also, we have learned about the close tribal and familial ties and obligations in Native American societies. There is great reverence among their people, as among ours, for the aged, for their knowledge and experience. Native American girls are taught from an early age to cook, sew, and help care for their younger siblings. Many are still painstakingly taught the beautiful, ancient art of beadwork and loom weaving.

It is interesting to note that in regard to acceptance of death, most Native Americans accept it as a natural part of life, and minister to the dying person, as well as revering the person's spirit after death. However, the Navaho tribe minister to the dying relative outside of the lodge, in the belief that demons associated with the *chindee* spirit will bring misfortune upon anyone who is close to the dying person, if it occurs inside the dwelling. This I learned from Riva Crawford, a knowledgeable member of the Shawnee tribe. In all Native American cultures, tribal unity is so strong that even if children are orphaned, other members of the tribe will take them and raise them.

Through the North American Indian Center of Boston, I have also come to know of the intense suffering and very unfair treatment given these people who are more American than anyone else in this country. Many Native American men get jobs in the construction industry, where their pay is often not equal to what Caucasians get, and where the hazards of the job are great. To maintain privacy, I shall use first names only. I got to know one very intelligent, dignified lady named Catherine, of the Micmac tribe, by way of her husband having been in a terrible accident on a construction job, from which he suffered multiple fractures and head injuries.

As Catherine came to my house, accompanied by friends, to pick up furniture donated to them (to which I added a chicken and a bag of potatoes), she unfolded her heart to me. In addition to her husband's having been in critical condition, he was almost totally blinded, and was on total bed rest. In great bitterness Catherine told me how she wanted to tear up the check of a few paltry dollars from Workmen's Compensation given to her husband. It was understandable, considering the maiming injuries he had sustained, in addition to her having to teach him speech all over again, because of the injury to his brain. Had she not taken a job on the night shift working for a caterer, plus a few handouts from other friends, Catherine would not even have been able to pay the rent for their tiny apartment. She was working her fingers practically to the bone. Notwithstanding her own agonies, Catherine hugged and kissed my daughter, Dalya, and called her *doss,* which means daughter in Micmac. We tearfully kissed each other good-bye, wishing each other's families the best of health and luck.

As for the language of the Native Americans, most of them are not illiterate, as most other Americans would like to believe. In addition to the Micmac language, which Catherine has been teaching to the younger generation of her people, the Cherokee Nation has a sophisticated language of its own, complete with a very advanced alphabet. The great Cherokee chief, John Ross, brought this to the attention of all of the United States about a century ago.

On the subject of Native Americans of great learning and valor, there are several great men of whom we learn from American history books, such as Pontiac, chief of the Ottawas, Osceola, the Seminole chief (whose tribe never signed a peace treaty with the American government), Sitting Bull, chief of the Lakota Sioux, who defeated General Custer at the Battle of Little Big Horn, and Chief John Ross, already mentioned.

There have also been several Native American women of great courage and wisdom. They contributed greatly to their people, as well as to American progress, in general. I am grateful to Margaret Truman Daniels, from whose book *Women of Courage* I have acquired some of this knowledge. Specifically, she wrote of one Thocmetony (Shell Flower), of the Southern Paiutes, who inhabited the area we now call Nevada. Due to ethnic clashes caused by an Indian agent called Rinehart, the Bannock tribe kidnapped the Southern Paiutes. Thocmetony (who took the English name Sarah) was asked by General O. O. Howard to act as a scout to help him rescue her people from the Bannock, which she did, riding over a hundred miles alone and then crawling up a steep mountain to reach her father. With the help of General Howard, Thocmetony succeeded in rescuing her people and returning to their Malheur reservation. After years of discourse with the United States Senate, Thocmetony got them to permanently give Malheur to her people.[1] She was a great lady in American history.

Another great Native American lady, Sacagawea, was the Shoshone woman who was instrumental in making the Lewis and Clark expedition a success. She was kidnapped by Minetarees as a child and given as a prize to a white man named Charbonneau, who took her as his wife and became a member of the expedition. Sacagawea helped them to reach the Pacific Ocean, notwithstanding a very difficult childbirth and many illnesses and hardships of the great journey from the Missouri River to the Pacific. There was one time when Sacagawea saved the expedition. They were all in a boat heading up the Missouri when the boat almost capsized. As most of the maps, charts, medicines, and scientific instruments were washed overboard, Sacagawea, holding her baby in one arm, retrieved these materials with the other arm, as they floated by. She had saved the expedition from ruin.[2] Moreover, she served as interpreter with her brother, chief Cah-me-ah-wait, once they reached Shoshone territory, to procure more horses for their trip. A few years after the expedition was completed, around 1812, Sacagawea died very prematurely. She was a very fine, brave lady to whom this country owes much.

Fortunately there have arisen in this generation Native Americans who are leading their people to a much brighter future. One such man is Wendell Chino, executive officer of the Mescalero Apaches, and descendant of the famous chief, Geronimo (correct name Goyatla). The name Mescalero comes from the Spanish word for an agave cactus plant, which tastes something like sweet potato and is what the tribe subsists on, together with other vegetables and bison meat.

Chino made a commitment to his people when he was a boy. He said, "When I grow up, I would like to do something about their living conditions, the hovels that were homes, all the poverty and disease I saw existing among my people." As leader of the tribe for over thirty-five years, Mr. Chino has seen to it that his people now live in a community with clean, pumped-in running water, cottages with gardens, and a fifteen-bed hospital. Hitherto there had been wretched shacks, illnesses such as tuberculosis and trachoma, and a high infant mortality rate.

This progress resulted from Chino's acquiring, in 1963, a ski resort on Sierra Blanca in the Sacramento Mountains outside the reservation. He got the necessary loan from the Bureau of Indian Affairs. Also, an artificial lake for fish breeding was acquired with the help of Stewart Udall, then Secretary of the Interior. From the million-and-a-half-dollar loan and investment, the project not only has been repaid, but turned into a twenty-five-million-dollar business. The place has been renamed Ski Apache. Here some of the wealthiest businessmen come from Texas to enjoy the ultra-modern hotel, private balconies, the lake, tennis courts, riding stable, and wild game hunting, the elk having been brought in by Mr. Udall from Yellowstone National Park. As a result of these undertakings, not only did the general lifestyle of the Mescaleros improve, but by the late 1980's about a hundred students were enrolled in colleges and vocational schools. Also, Mescaleros are now trained and given jobs at Ski Apache or the local timber business or the new sawmill run by the tribe.

On the subject of culture, there is an unwritten Athabascan language that the Apaches speak, as their original tongue. Also, in regard to culture, the greatest Mescalero Apache holiday, which is celebrated around July 4 each year, is the five-day Maidens' Puberty Rights Ceremony. In it are certain running activities around baskets of Apache talismans, with the young ladies who are coming of age very carefully dressed, massaged, and tended by their grandmothers and godmothers. Attired in buckskin tunics and trousers that are adorned with exquisite beadwork and stitching, they kneel and prostrate themselves on buckskins. This ceremony is intended to ensure healthy families for the tribe. Many neighboring tribes often celebrate this ceremony with the Mescaleros, which also includes the men's Dance of the Mountain Gods, in full attire. This dance is supposed to drive away illness and evil and bring good health and luck.[3]

Though I have never been present at such a Mescalero Apache ceremony, my daughter and I took part in a pow-wow, or gathering of the different tribal members of the Boston Indian Council, in the summer of 1988. During this pow-wow we saw dances of various tribes, the men being beautifully outfitted in trouser and tunic suits heavily embroidered with hand beadwork and colorful feather trimmings. These men, playing drums and tambourines, were in the innermost circle. The bedecked husband and wife teams, followed by their children, made the next circle around the male dancers, and any others, including non-Native Americans, formed the outermost circle of dancers. There was a separate dance performed by the young women, who wore heavily fringed shawls in beautiful bright colors over their native suits, and who danced in a graceful, bird-like fashion. My daughter and I had the honor of helping with the cooking and other kitchen work for the pow-wow. Then we joined the dancers. In short, a beautiful, cultural afternoon was had by all.

Through my membership in the American Indian College Fund, I have come to be acquainted with several families of the Sioux nation in

South Dakota. I became acquainted with Iris Between Lodges, who lives in the Oglala area of the Pine Ridge reservation, whose Shannon County is one of the most poverty-stricken counties in the entire United States. I also came to know Dr. Agnes Picotte and husband, Norbert Picotte, who reside in Chamberlain, South Dakota. Agnes holds a Doctorate in Philosophy and Native American Languages, but is a very humble woman. Both Picottes are charming people.

The author with Dr. Agnes Picotte and her husband, Norbert, at their home in Chamberlain, South Dakota, March 1996.

Knowing that I alone would not be able to further the Native American cause, I turned to the late Massachusetts Congressman John J. Moakley, who said he would be glad to try to seek political support for my trip to Pine Ridge, and asked me to return to him for a debriefing upon completing the trip. Certain friends supported me financially for the trip, and then I went ahead with my plans with Iris and the Picottes to provide lodging and transportation for me once I arrived there. I was also educated by a lady who had had previous contacts with the Sioux on what to say and what not to say when among the Sioux people. I was told never to bring a tape recorder or writing pad. After being warmly received (though several hours late) by the Picottes at Sioux City and driven home with them to board with them, a young Sioux woman and her family picked me up next morning for the five-hour drive to Pine Ridge. They were extremely affable with me, and even drove me to the heart-wrenching cemetery at Wounded Knee. There the United States Cavalry had massacred over three hundred unarmed Sioux, mostly old people, women, and children, with a few braves, in 1895.[4] I felt the blood go cold in my spine and my fists clench involuntarily as I stood at the entrance to the monument. There stood only a cross above a small brick gate to mark the place. Finally my driver brought me to the center of Pine Ridge, where the Director then was Malcolm Lone Hill, who also greeted me very warmly. One of his first questions was, "Would you like a pad of writing paper?" Then, as I told him what I wasn't supposed to say, we both burst out laughing. Malcolm proceeded to inform me with as much material as he could about area in miles and population at the reservation, high infant mortality rate, severe overcrowding in inadequate housing, resulting in high rates of active tuberculosis and other infectious diseases. He also informed me about the high incidence of alcoholism, which is due partly to a gene that is defective in some Native Americans, so that they cannot tolerate alcohol. Then Malcolm went ahead to arrange an appointment for me to go to the local hospital at Pine Ridge a couple of days later.

In the meantime, though I was originally supposed to stay at the convent in Pine Ridge, I ended up becoming the guest of Iris Between Lodges, who told her daughter, Nora, to give me her bedroom, which I said wasn't really necessary, but Iris and Nora insisted. Iris had ten children and was one of the poorest people on the reservation, but insisted on treating me like a queen. I was most deeply touched by their respect for my religion. When I asked Nora if it would be all right for me to bless the Sabbath candles on the table, she said it would be fine, and the six-year-old told the five-year-old, "We mustn't touch that till Saturday night, because it's Saralea's sacred fire to the Jewish *Wakantanka*." The Sioux name for the Great Spirit is Wakantanka, whom we call G-d. In no other gentile home was I ever shown such respect. Of course I brought my own tuna fish and yogurt, and was singularly provoked when Iris went to pay the cashier, who took the money, threw it to the floor, and said, "Pick it up, Injun." There was still discrimination there, even in February of 1996, which was the date of my trip. One day, when Iris had a day off from work, she decided to drive me around the reservation, and then to the Red Cloud Indian School, which is still run by Jesuits. She introduced me to the priest in charge and then showed me all around the school.

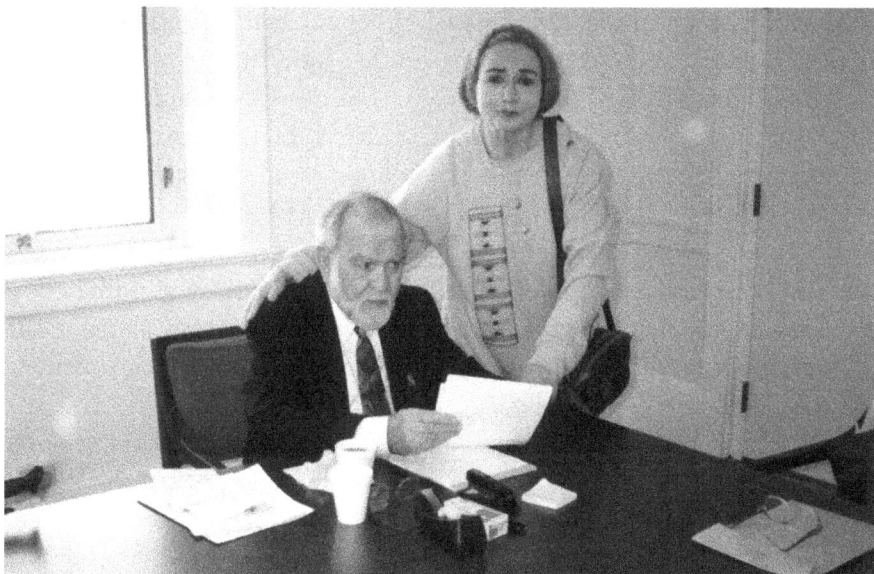

Massachusetts Congressman John J. Moakley with the author for a debriefing after her trip to the Pine Ridge reservation in South Dakota, March 1996.

When I was preparing to leave South Dakota, a terrible blizzard came up, and Iris, with nerves of steel, decided to drive me half way to Agnes Picotte's sister's home in Kyle. There was about twenty yards' visibility. Barton Merrival, Agnes's brother-in-law, met me half way to Kyle with Norbert in the car. I paid Iris, of course, and we agreed that when I got home I'd send her coats for her children and grandchildren. Evangeline and Barton Merrival treated me like family completely, except that Agnes, who was quite upset that they drove me in the storm, rattled on in Sioux, of which I understood not a word. They did give me a gift of a handmade key chain made of leather strips and Indian beadwork, which was their way of saying "Thank you" to me. It was given to me in the spirit of the "potlatch," which among Native Americans indicates one's greatness, not in acquiring riches, but in giving to those who have less than we do.

Though I kept in touch with Iris (and her sister, Karen, whom I've not yet mentioned) for several years and sent her all the coats plus some personal gifts, a young man answered the phone in 2002 who said he knew nothing of them. Agnes and Norbert Picotte and I have kept steadfastly in touch, especially remembering each other at Christmas and Chanukah, with gifts and cards, and phoning each other from time to time. My new name in Sioux is Tchane Omanee Wee, or Walks Far Woman. Also, very importantly, thanks to the diligence of the late Congressman Moakley, two hundred model homes with indoor plumbing and central heating, plus refrigerators, have been erected at Pine Ridge. My efforts for a recreation center under the guidance of SuAnne Big Crow were not in vain, as one has just been erected in Pine Ridge, and I've been soliciting funds for it, as I was requested. Now the young men have something better to do than get drunk; it's also under supervision, and has an indoor toilet and drinking fountain.

In general, the lot of the average Native American has been a severe one. In the words of one Penobscot friend of mine, "Perhaps Christopher Columbus did not do the greatest thing in discovering America." The Native people took only what they needed from the land, and returned the rest to the land. Since the Europeans came to America, they have ravaged the land, and have destroyed more ecological balance than can be counted, to the point in many cases that the damage has become irreversible. It is only in recent years, with the presentation of Kevin Kostner's film *Dances with Wolves,* and more recently the film *Geronimo,* with a Native American, Wes Studi, playing the lead role, that proper recognition of true Native American values, culture, and dignity has begun to emerge. When more Native Americans acquire college degrees, which will enable them to begin to take the helm in American professional life, only then will the desperate situation of racial inequality in the United States begin to be rectified. It is for this reason that we must strive diligently to support the American Indian College Fund, which now has thirty-two colleges, with colleges on each of the reservations. Once many of the students get their degrees in nursing, social service, and engineering, they return to the reservations to help better their people's lives. Several are now studying to be astronauts. Others have become physicians, to serve their people's health needs on the reservations. For as long as my energy is needed to serve the Native American cause, especially the American Indian College Fund, I shall be there to serve my adopted people.

SIX

LIVING AND LEARNING IN ISRAEL

ORIGINALLY, TOGETHER WITH MANY OTHER JEWISH VOLUNTEERS, I HAD INTENDED TO GO TO ISRAEL DURING THE 1967 WAR, BUT AS THE ISRAELIS TOLD US NOT TO COME, I PUT OFF MY TRIP TILL MAY OF 1968. It was just as well, because at the time I spoke no Hebrew and had a minimal knowledge of triage. My cousins, Rachel, Ida, Avram, Lola, Shoshanna, and Adrian, had been excitedly planning for this trip with me, and Rachel and Avram met me at Haifa harbor. They took me back by taxi to Nahariya, where they live. We communicated freely in Yiddish, which was my mother tongue as well as theirs.

Nahariya is the most picturesque city in Israel (besides Jerusalem), with its arches that span the brook in the center of town. There were mini-malls with shoe stores, jewelry and souvenir stores, a butcher shop, and ice cream parlors. Each mall was neatly laid out with flower gardens and benches. Horse-drawn carriages for hire added an Old World effect. Nahariya was settled primarily by Jews from Germany (and later Romania), the German Jews being known for their lovely trellised gardens, and for straightforward prices. You have to haggle with most vendors in Israel and the Middle East, but not with the *Yekkis,* as the German and Czechoslovakian Jews are called.

I had a beautiful reception at my Aunt Esther's and Cousin Rachel's homes, with all the family, including my younger cousins, Miki, Yoli, Gila, Miriam, and Bracha welcoming me to Israel. Here I was introduced to Israeli coffee, in which you allow about an inch of gritty residue to settle before you drink it. I was also introduced to *hummus* (a thick puree made of mashed chickpeas, seasoned with garlic, lemon juice, and spices, and blended with *tehina,* a paste made of ground sesame seeds), which is eaten with *pita,* a flat Middle Eastern bread, tomatoes, and cucumbers. After eating and catching up on family information, we all went for a stroll up to the seashore. Nahariya has a large, beautiful beach, and every Yom Shabbat (Saturday, the day of rest), we all took off for the seashore. Nahariya is semi-urban and semi-pastoral.

My late Aunt Esther's and Uncle Isaac's one-room, hewn-stone apartment was an education to me, with the bed, sofa, table and chairs, and refrigerator all tucked into the main room, off of which extended the tiny kitchen and shower-stall bathroom. There was a small, rear balcony also. It made me reflect on how spoiled I was, coming from American affluence.

In the process of visiting with various relatives, I got to stay with my Aunt Jeanette and Uncle Chaim in Netanya. On one Shabbat, Aunt Jeanette took me to synagogue with her. It was during the holiday of Shavuot, which celebrates the giving of the Torah (Hebrew law). All the ladies had on simple dresses, and all of them wore kerchiefs. I was greeted enthusiastically in Yiddish by all the ladies, as my Aunt Jeanette introduced me to them as her niece newly arrived from America. I was assailed by questions from all sides, as to how I came to speak Yiddish so well, whether I intended to make my home in Israel, and whether I would be a guest in their homes. It is customary during Shavuot for friends and relatives to visit, at which time dairy dishes and fruits are served.

Also, the Book of Ruth is read, to commemorate Ruth, the Moabitess, accepting the Torah and Judaism as her own faith. Here is exemplified the great inspiration that Naomi gave her daughter-in-law, Ruth, to leave the land of abundance and follow a bereaved mother-in-law to a strange land and religion. Ruth became one of the great mothers in Hebrew history, as the wife of Joab. Their grandson was to be David, King of Israel.

The Ashkenazi ladies of the congregation cordially shared their meager fare with me. In addition, my aunt later introduced me to her Moroccan Jewish neighbors, who invited me to visit and share the holiday with them, also. My aunt's neighbors had little, as their homes were sparsely furnished and the ladies wore outdated dresses that were most likely given them as refugees to the country. Some of them had barely enough to get by on, but it meant so much to them to lay out their best for a sister Jewess from abroad.

The Moroccan Jewesses also taught me about the marriage custom of Hazala. On the day of the wedding, the bride is dressed in a floor-length, long-sleeved dress of white brocade decorated with gold or silver metallic embroidery. The bridesmaids wear similar dresses of different-colored brocade. On the second day of the wedding, the bride and groom are seated on adjacent high-backed chairs, with the men beating on Oriental drums and the girls dancing around them. The groom wears a white satin shirt and white baggy trousers gathered at the waist with a cummerbund, while the bride wears the traditional white head cloth, and a long white linen dress cinched at the waist. Both the bride and the groom wear red velvet vests decorated with gold metallic designs. A *kiddush* (blessing) is recited over the wine, and cakes are served as well. I witnessed one such ritual of Hazala and found it rich with ethnic, Jewish refinement.

There was another experience that I remember distinctly from the time I stayed with my Aunt Jeanette and Uncle Chaim in Netanya. I was returning to their home from a bus trip, and it happened to be during a severe rainstorm. In those days the Shicun (area) Dora section was all sandy and unpaved, and it turned into a quagmire in bad weather. From the edge of town I decided to try to hitchhike home, as the wait for the local bus could be very long. In a short while a jeep pulled up, driven by a dark brown skinned, middle-aged man with grayish black hair. He looked respectable and said that he was going in my direction, so I should feel free to join him. He introduced himself as a married Iraqi Jew with three sons, all of whom were grown up. I told him where I came from and that I was visiting with family in Netanya. He told me in Hebrew, "Welcome to our Jewish homeland and be blessed." I had the feeling that he was driving out of his way and offered him some money for gasoline. At this he absolutely refused to accept anything and said, "Perhaps if I have been kind to you, G-d will see to it that others will be kind to my children." I was so deeply touched by this generosity from a total stranger, as well as his gentlemanliness. It was events such as these that made me feel that I was at home in Israel, though I'd been there only a few months.

As for the rest of my first stay in Israel, my cousins Rachel and Mircha, Ida and Tsvi, and Kutsa and Avram were very hospitable in taking turns putting me up till I got to try out life for a couple of months in Kibbutz Farod in Upper Galilee. The kibbutz was one of a number of kibbutzim and Arab villages that are close to Lake Kinneret (Sea of Galilee). To the south of it lies Jordan, to the west the famed resort city of Tiberias, to the east Kibbutz Ein Gev and the Arab village of Aqab, and to the north the town of Rosh Pina. Also to the north is the city of Tsvat (Safed), famous for its artists' quarter, as well as the ancient seat of learning of Kabbala (Kabbala being the profound book of Hebrew mysticism). Also to the north is Kuneitra, whose kibbutz withstood more merciless battering by Syria in all the Arab-Israeli wars than any other single kibbutz.

I found Lake Kinneret to be one of the most beautiful places I have ever seen. Its clear, blue waters mirrored the light blue sky, interspersed with fluffy, white clouds. This, combined with the majestic beauty of the Jordanian mountains to the south and the Lebanese mountains to the north, with dew covering their brown and purple tops, is exquisite.

The first couple of weeks at Kibbutz Farod took some getting used to, and a number of us new volunteers made ridiculous blunders. On time off from class and work, another young woman volunteer and I decided to take a bus trip to Tsvat. As the bus pulled up at the stop, we realized that we hadn't brought any money. We both then brightly exclaimed, *"Ain lanukelev liknot kartees, ain kelev,"* which translated into Hebrew was, "We do not have dogs with which to buy a ticket, no dogs." At this the driver slammed the doors on us and drove onward. A native kibbutznik standing alongside of us tried to explain to us, with a little Hebrew and sign language, "See friends, *kelev* is woof, woof; *kesev* is here," pointing to the palm of his hand.

As we blundered through mistakes in Hebrew, and also adjustments to climate, clothing, and communal-style lodging, we found the people of the kibbutz very accommodating. They showed us around and invited us to their tiny cabins after work hours. This was invaluable, as many of the kibbutznikim had come from the same countries as we had, so they were able to speak our languages fluently. For those of us who, like myself, spoke Yiddish, the language adjustment was much easier, as most of the kibbutz members had come from Eastern Europe and also spoke Yiddish.

While in Kibbutz Farod I made a number of friends. The closest of these was a fellow public health nurse from Finland, Eva Cecilia. She was slim, with fair skin and straight blond hair. Eva Cecilia spoke English fluently, and she and I teamed up, on occasion, with another volunteer, Una, from France. Una, unfortunately, spoke no English, and she found Hebrew extremely difficult to learn. Thus Eva Cecelia and I resorted to sign language with Una.

One day after our *ulpan* (intensive Hebrew) study and field work were done, the three of us decided to traipse off to a Sephardi café about a mile up the road to treat ourselves to some beer. This was during a severe heat wave. After arriving at the cafe we each ordered three beers, in succession. There is a particular Israeli brown beer that is very rich, and Eva Cecilia, Una, and I guzzled down bottle after bottle. Suddenly a huge belch erupted from me. The café owner immediately responded in Hebrew with, "Bless you, child, bless you," as the other customers looked on approvingly. It is the custom in the Middle East, when someone belches, to bless him or her. I felt appalled. To rub it in, Eva Cecelia had to chime in, "Yes, bless you, child, bless you," as she laughed her head off. Then we left to return to the kibbutz.

By now our heads were swimming, and the road seemed to sway back and forth in front of us. A pit viper, driven out of its burrow by the intense heat, suddenly slithered by our path. Una said in French, "Let's catch that string." As we bent over to grab it, it sped away into the underbrush. Most snakes are endowed with the ability to travel at great speed. Luckily for us, it got away. The bite of a viper is extremely venomous, and it can kill unless anti-venom is administered promptly. We continued to flounder back to our cabins, and finally collapsed onto our beds. We each had a long nap after that.

There were other escapades that Eva Cecilia and I enjoyed on our days off together. One of them was the time we hitchhiked with a fellow kibbutznik to Nahariya. We had a limited mount of money with us, so we couldn't afford to spend too much. After doing some window-shopping at jewelry and clothing shops, we decided to go into the local supermarket. Israeli supermarkets are very sophisticated by Western standards, with display cases very clean and attractive. They offer a variety of fruits, vegetables, meats, fowl, and bottled drinks. We were both getting quite hungry by now, and as we passed the fresh fish section, Eva Cecelia grabbed two tiny fish and chucked them both into her mouth. I had all I could do to prevent myself from bursting out laughing.

After that we managed to find a *falafel* stand, where we each ordered a pita bread filled with falafel, tomatoes, and cucumbers and topped with delicious tehina sauce. Falafel is made from ground-up raw chickpeas, combined with garlic, onions, and semolina, rolled into balls, and boiled in hot oil for about twenty minutes. It's a highly nutritious vegetarian dish, very inexpensive, and is served at restaurants and roadside stands throughout the Middle East.

The balmy afternoon air of Nahariya was filled with the fragrance of flowers and the aroma of Turkish coffee. Both sides of the main street, with the brook in the center, were harmoniously tree-lined. Before dusk, Eva Cecelia and I discreetly hitchhiked with another kibbutznik, had a pleasant though bumpy ride home, and thanked the kibbutznik for the lift.

In Israel it is not considered as dangerous to hitchhike as it is in the United States. Nevertheless, I would not advise a woman to try it alone, especially after dark, as occasional rapes, beatings, and even killings by Arabs disguised as Jews have been known to occur. It is the expected, courteous thing for Israelis driving a car with room to spare to pick up male and female soldiers who are waiting by the roadside. This is uniquely so in Israel, because just about every married couple there has children who are in or who have been in the military, so it's a matter of everyone's caring about everyone else's children. This occurs throughout Israel.

Before I left kibbutz life, I learned from another foreign volunteer about some interesting customs among Arab people. Marion was becoming engaged to a young Arab, so she was invited to visit with him and his family in Akko. After the meal and some light conversation, Marion's future sisters-in-law brought her to the bath. After helping Marion to disrobe, the young women insisted on helping her to wash and dry her body, and then dress her, starting by putting her bra and pants on her.

Marion was at a total loss for words. Then one of the women explained to her that since she was about to become one of the family, bathing and dressing her was a part of the welcoming ceremony. Marion said afterwards to Eva Cecelia and me that she could never accustom herself to this total lack of privacy. It is also accepted in all Middle Eastern societies that as part of the marriage ritual, after the marriage is consummated, elder aunts of the groom examine the bed sheets for blood, as proof of the bride's being a virgin. This may seem gross to people of the West, but maintenance of virginity is a must in religious Middle Eastern culture.

Also, I have heard it said by Westerners visiting with Arabs or Jews, especially Sephardi Jews, that we are hyper-reactive in our greetings. Among Semites, when we welcome a friend or relative, it is considered proper etiquette for the men of the family to hug and kiss a male guest on both cheeks, and for the women of the family to do likewise with a female guest. Semites are simply very demonstrative people.

To return to kibbutz life, though I enjoyed the communal sharing, the permissiveness was not for me, so after two months on the kibbutz, I applied for and was accepted into Ulpan Etzion in Jerusalem. This was then Israel's leading immigrant education center. We had an excellent education under the leadership of headmaster Dr. Mordecai Kamarat. He and our class teacher, Chava Yuran, had immense patience with us, many of whom had never before heard a word of Hebrew, and came from many different countries.

There were four of us to a dormitory room, with the exception of the married couples' rooms, which were of course private. In my dormitory room, for example, in addition to myself, there was Eugenia, a dentist from Argentina; Rivka, a school teacher from England; and Aliza, a medical student at the University of Jerusalem, to whom I was closest and to whom I shall soon refer again. As good fortune would have it, we could all speak Yiddish to some extent, and all of us in my dorm room were mutually considerate of each other. Thus, in spite of lack of adequate closet space and privacy, we made a very good go of it. We all helped each other with our Hebrew lessons. We made such mistakes as calling grapes "people," with one consonant misplaced. The other mistakes were hilarious, such as the one where in the dining room, instead of asking for *gezer*, which means carrot, we asked for *gever mevushal*, which means cooked men. Our table was referred to from then on as the table where the cannibals sat.

In our class alone, there were Jews from Iran, Morocco, Switzerland, Italy, the United States, France, and England, as well as a Protestant nurse from Finland. Most of us students were professionals, and caught on adequately to reading, writing, and speaking Hebrew. A few, mostly non-Jews from Scandinavia, found it very difficult, and made limited progress in their Hebrew lessons. We must keep in mind that the Hebrew alphabet, though it forms the basis of many Indo-European languages, is in written or printed form very different from the alphabets of other languages, and so for anyone brought up to know one language only, the transition is very difficult.

The climate was another thing to which many could not adjust, in particular to the intense heat of summer, without any fans or air conditioners in our dorms or classrooms. For me the hot weather with thirty percent humidity made for comfortable living. There were also frequent electric power outages in the district, though this has long since been corrected. Especially for those of us who got jobs working at night, flashlights were indispensable.

This was back in 1968, when the State of Israel had limited resources, so some basic items had to be rationed, which upset some of the Western students, used to the luxuries of life in their native lands. Meat was served once in a day, with the basic food staples being rice, potatoes, and a good variety of vegetables, fruits, and dairy products. Cake was served on the Sabbath.

Though we were at first allowed to shower nightly, because of water shortages we were subsequently restricted to weekly showers. I found that if we really sponge-bathed properly daily and used deodorants and talc, weekly showers could suffice. Some students raised a hue and cry about this restriction, though. People have to try to understand what life in a pioneering land is all about, including sacrifices.

Moreover, the cleaning and kitchen staff of mostly Moroccan Jews, whose privations had been far greater than ours, overextended themselves to accommodate us. When they had first come to Israel in the early 1950's, they had had to live in tents, quite often with snakes and other reptiles slithering in, especially during rainstorms, when the ground in the tents turned into a sea of mud. There was no way to keep warm, unless they were lucky enough to get a good wood fire going. Consequently, many of these North African Jews became afflicted with tuberculosis and malaria. They certainly did not get to shower every night, or eat meat even once in a day.

Their medical facilities included one immigrant doctor or nurse, together with whatever supplies they could muster, such as some bandages, antiseptics, morphine for pain, aspirin, and antibiotics donated to them by other settlers who'd preceded them. All drinking water had to be boiled, as most of it from local wells, water holes, and streams was potentially septic. There were even a few mild outbreaks of cholera. Some of the settlers did not survive all of these hardships. The memories of these brave, industrious people who suffered so much to pave the way for the rest of us must not be forgotten.

It was here that I had my first contact with Palestinians through my roommate, Aliza. She introduced me to a Palestinian Arab named Mahmoud, a medical student, and to several of his friends, also students at the University of Jerusalem Medical School. They were all very polite to me, though their resentment, somewhat masked, of an intruder into what they considered their land was obvious.

Through Aliza I was introduced to another aspect of Jewish life, that of the European Jews who had suffered. Aliza and her mother, father, sister, and brother had traveled from their native Galicia to Uruguay and then Israel. The worst suffering was that of Aliza's brother-in-law, who had been one of the children on the famed ship *Exodus*. He was on the ship with a combined leg fracture and ulceration, which never properly healed. This was while the British held the ship at sea, not permitting it to sail into port in Palestine, until weeks later. Years later, after he and Aliza's sister had married, he still suffered from pain and disability in the injured leg. He managed to work, nevertheless, at a menial job, to maintain his dignity.

It was while I was a guest at their house in Kiryat Chaim in Haifa that I was introduced to the whole family, all of whom were very hospitable to me. Except for Aliza's brother and brother-in-law, everyone else was on the stocky side. Aliza herself was tall and quite attractive, with wavy, dark brown hair, dark brown eyes, and a slightly hooked nose over well-set lips. Although given to mood swings, she was basically a good-humored person.

The wear and tear of all the international moves and poverty showed more strongly on Aliza's parents, both of whom were prematurely gray-haired. Nonetheless, they welcomed me with spontaneous warmth and generosity. Though they were not well educated, they easily shifted back and forth from Hebrew to Yiddish and Spanish during our conversation. As I recall, Aliza's sister worked as a licensed practical nurse and essentially had the same features as Aliza. As she came home from work and collapsed into a chair, she grabbed for a piece of leftover *kishka* (to be described shortly), and began munching on it. This type of food probably accounted for the family's stockiness, as it's quite high in calories. Aliza's brother, Chaim, was home from the army for a few precious days.

It was obvious that materially the family had little. Aliza and I slept in a single bed opposite the place where her parents slept, and her sister and brother-in-law slept in an alcove with a curtain over it, while Aliza's brother slept on the couch in the tiny parlor. The day after I arrived, the family included me in the kitchen to watch them making kishka—sheep's intestine cleaned and stuffed with a savory filling of flour, rendered chicken fat, and onions and spices. I have always enjoyed it, freshly roasted from the oven. We had vegetable soup, salad, and noodle pudding, too. The space was crowded and the furnishings were plain, but the homey atmosphere and generosity made up for it. I was accepted into Aliza's household as if I were a member of the family. I think that much credit is due them all, and Aliza in particular, as I later learned that she had achieved her much-desired degree in medicine and psychiatry.

There was one last, gripping moment that I experienced with Aliza's family, with everyone at the supper table. Chaim had to leave for his post in the army. Knowing well that Chaim might never return again, Aliza's mother said good-bye to him with her face drawn and her gaze cast down on the table in front of her. It is not only the three years of active military service that each soldier must undergo, but also the month out of each year thereafter, during which he must serve in the reserves. Thus a soldier's completing his or her two to three years in the Israeli armed forces does not automatically provide a respite from the military. So small and beleaguered a nation must be on constant stand-by alert.

Some fellow Americans have said to me, "Being in the Israeli military, always on call-up, must make many Israelis want to leave Israel." In some cases this is true. However, this is another reason that makes us proud of being Jewish—caring and fighting side by side. The thought of having our own land from which no Cossacks or anti-Jewish Muslims can chase us is as precious as life. My ex-husband was shot once in the back and once in the right arm, with a shrapnel wound that has left a partial hole in his arm. Many friends and relatives of ours who lost children in the Arab-Israeli wars, though they bear permanent heartaches, feel that Israel is still dear to them.

As students at Ulpan Etzion, we were all taken out on occasional excursions. By far the most riveting one was to Kibbutz Lochamai HaGetaot, the kibbutz comprised of survivors of the Warsaw Ghetto in the Second World War. The kibbutz was located halfway up the main road that extends from Nahariya to Haifa, in northern Israel. We went in summer, so everyone wore short sleeves, and the concentration camp numbers tattooed onto all the kibbutz members' arms put us on immediate notice that these people had survived the death camps.

At the entrance to the kibbutz museum was a sign printed in Hebrew and in English: "Never to forget, never to forgive." Even Yad Vashem, the Holocaust Memorial in Jerusalem, did not possess such an unforgettable array of the tragic memorabilia of the subhuman atrocities to which the Jews were subjected in the death camps. There were pictures of men, women, and children stripped naked, starved, and tortured by enucleations, burns, and beatings. There were also photos of Jews with their arms twisted and wrenched behind their backs, or hanging by their wrists from trees. This was as punishment for infractions such as having stolen a piece of stale bread or not having been able to complete their camp workload. We were told that thousands of these poor souls were left to hang from trees till their arms were wrenched out of their shoulder sockets. They were then left to rot there, or cut down from the trees and beaten to death by SS men with rifle butts.

At Kibbutz Lochamai HaGetaot there were, of course, pictures of the gigantic mass graves where Jews were machine-gunned to death, and then were thrown in. Some were very much alive, though wounded, with the blood and excrement of fellow Jews' bodies pouring over them.

The examples of atrocity that gripped us worst were the glass-enclosed galvanized baby booties and shoes. These had belonged to the infants whom Ilse Koch and her evil female cohorts had impaled on bayonets. I believe that it was this that caused Mama Tzipah to say to me as she lay on her deathbed that she no longer believed in G-d. She said that had He existed, He would have smitten the Nazis with lightning bolts as they perpetrated these horrors.

These thoughts have burned themselves indelibly into my mind, and I have shared them freely with my daughter since she became thirteen years old. At this age she was mature enough to be able to comprehend and appreciate these grim historical facts, and never forget the meaning of the suffering of our people (and of all victims of genocide). Together with me, Dalya watched, with tears in her eyes, the Holocaust documentaries that were presented on television station WGBH-TV during 1988 and 1989. It's important to me that she never become insensitive to the suffering of others, as so many have about the genocide against Native Americans, the Nazi Holocaust, and the murder of millions of innocent Cambodians by the Pol Pot regime.

Aside from the grim reminders of the past, through Ulpan Etzion we were also taken to the ruins of King Herod's palace and the man-made harbor at Cesarea. Though King Herod was known for his great cruelty, nevertheless this was a supreme architectural feat, remaining from over two thousand years ago. The remnants of perfectly constructed metal and stone drinking systems and closed, separate sewage systems, together with floors of exquisite tiles, were stupendous. The aqueducts were large enough to serve a small city. There we also saw beautifully made pottery fragments and oil lamps to illuminate the city.

One hilarious event took place on our ride back to Ulpan Etzion. A young man panicked as he needed to get off at the Tel Aviv bus stop and shouted, *"Ani tsarich laledet,"* which is Hebrew for "I have to give birth." He meant to say *laredet,* which means "to descend or get down." We all broke out laughing for a good ten minutes after that, and ribbed Matthew afterwards for a good few weeks about his "giving birth."

Several months later, Aliza and our other classmates and I graduated from Ulpan Etzion. After completing ulpan, I decided to try my fortune at getting a job in nursing, plus an apartment. Ultimately, I got a job as a public health nurse in Tsvat, with a communal apartment to go with it. The other nurses and I shared it, including cooking, toilet, and sleeping facilities. Here I was taught by Shoshanna, a Yemenite supervisor who was one of the brightest nurses I have ever met. She was the daughter of a rabbi and had married an Ashkenazi Jew. Shoshanna was slim and about five feet three inches tall, with medium brown skin (similar to my future husband's complexion), vivacious dark brown eyes, and jet-black hair pulled into a pony tail. She and her two Yemenite co-workers, Yona and Madi, gave me a cordial welcome to their public health unit, offering me coffee and cake right away, then orienting me to the nurses' room, the examination rooms, the blood laboratory, and the immunization equipment.

The Yemenite Jews are very open, pious, and extremely well educated in Hebraic laws and customs. It was here that I was first impressed by the great warmth and generosity of Yemenite Jewish society. Shoshanna showed me great understanding and taught me many medical techniques, including baby deliveries, immunizations, and laboratory tests. I learned well from her, Yona, and Madi. Shoshanna tolerated my inadequate Hebrew also, considering that all medical orders, reports, and records, were kept in Hebrew. On occasion, one of the foreign doctors would write up a patient's history in English and Latin. I would often make mistakes in the records because my Hebrew was not that good. Shoshanna, Madi, and Yona had lots of fun, too, telling all sorts of jokes, including some off-color ones, when we were on break from patient care. These nurses also gave a great deal of attention to every patient in our clinics, whether the patients were Jewish or Arab, literate or illiterate. We made a good team in our public health clinics.

While among the Yemenite Jews, I had an opportunity to learn about some fascinating ethnic customs. The Yemenite Jewish wedding, for example, lasts for two weeks. Just before the wedding, the bride's and groom's hands are stained with red henna, which is used to drive off the evil eye. The bride is then carefully dressed by a Yemenite Jewess specially skilled in it. She is dressed in the ritual tunic, dress, and headdress (described in Chapter Eleven).

The Yemenite Jewish customs are steeped in religion. The *chamsa* (a silver filigreed piece made to look like an upside-down hand) is a representation of the hand of G-d watching over the Jewish people. The chamsa is one of the many blessings that are hung up on the walls of most Sephardi and many Ashkenazi homes in Israel and elsewhere.

As for the rest of the Yemenite Jewish wedding, the religious ceremony itself is held under the *chupah* (four wooden posts with a canopy covering them, representing the canopy of heaven). The elders and grandparents of the bride dance the first dance with the bride, a kind of forward-and-backward dance step. The food, which includes a large variety of hotly spiced meats cooked in soup, and breads, also heavily spiced, is uniquely Yemenite. They are delicious, notwithstanding the heartburn. After the wedding, friends and relatives visit the newlyweds at their home and present gifts to them. They also visit the homes of the bride's and groom's parents to wish them *mazaltov* ("good luck," in Hebrew) and to present gifts to them as well.

In some respects the Yemenite Jewish wedding is celebrated in the same way as all other Jewish weddings. The chupah is used in all Jewish wedding ceremonies, and among all Orthodox Jews the men and women dance separately. Also, under the chupah, at the end of the ceremony the groom steps on and breaks the wine glass from which he and the bride have just drunk *kiddush*. This act symbolizes the destruction of the original Temple in Jerusalem by the Romans. A *ketuba* (marriage contract) is usually drawn up by the groom, to provide for the bride in the event of separation or divorce.

Through my work as a public health nurse I also began learning about Druze culture. The Druze are members of an Arabic religious community who live mainly in the isolated mountainous areas of Syria and Lebanon, but also in Israel. I was first introduced to some members of this sect by way of Estee, another novice nurse who was training with me under the tutelage of Shoshanna Weinstein. Estee and her husband, Uri, lived in Kuneitra, the town closest to the Syrian border on the Golan Heights. Once in February of 1969, Estee and her husband invited me to spend the weekend with them at their kibbutz. Aside from the place being freezing cold in the vast open spaces of Kuneitra, I received the usual informal kibbutz hospitality in the communal dining hall and the cabins.

I was, in addition, unexpectedly treated to a spectacle: a dance performed by some Druzim from the neighboring village of Magdal

Shams who had been invited to an informal party given by the members of the kibbutz. Several Druze males, attired in turtleneck sweaters, trousers, and jackets, performed consecutively in what I would call a dagger dance, to the accompaniment of drums, tambourines, and flutes. The men danced with astonishing grace as they unsheathed their daggers from their scabbards, throwing them into the air and catching them hilt first. On occasion, two Druze men entered the dance circle together, doing the dances. The performance started at about nine in the evening and went on far into the night, with the younger Druze boys of about ages ten to fourteen watching as their elders danced on, seemingly tirelessly. Druze females were strictly forbidden to attend such parties.

I almost made the catastrophic mistake of patting a young Druze boy on the head, but Estee quickly pulled my arm back, telling me it is taboo for any woman other than a Druze family member to touch a Druze male. It could have caused a serious confrontation between the Druze community and the members of Kuneitra. It taught me a very worthwhile, quick lesson in Druze and Arab manners and protocol. In some cases the kibbutz men joined in with the Druzim. I was told that the Druze men were experts, in more ways than one, in the use of the knife, and that it was considered an honor for an Arab to die in battle with his sword or dagger still in his hand.

As for the Druze women, I was told that it was acceptable for them and the Druze girls to participate only in parties of other females, unless they were sitting in the background at a Druze festivity, and serving the males their food. I shall remember that outstanding night at Kuneitra, watching the Druze men perform their dagger dances, albeit with my teeth chattering throughout it all. It was worth every freezing moment of it!

Estee and I continued to enjoy a working relationship as nurses at the Israeli Ministry of Health, always learning something new from Shoshanna, Yoni, and Madi.

It was about this time when I was enjoying life in Israel that the news came from America that Mama Tzipah had been attacked, together with a friend, Sam Aaronson, and two African-American ladies, in a cab for the blind, in the Roxbury neighborhood of Boston. The attackers were African-American militants, and all the occupants of the cab, except for the driver, were at least partially blind, with their red and white canes.

Mama's friend, Samuel, died as a result of the injuries from that attack, and Mama was badly battered by the bricks, rocks, and bottles that were thrown at them. The other ladies were also badly injured. The cab driver was threatened, and the perpetrators were never apprehended.

How base and senseless can people be, when in their hatred they attack old, blind people? Once Mama Tzipah had recovered sufficiently from her injuries, she said she felt sorry for the perpetrators, as they must have been treated very badly most of their lives. Thus I returned to the United States to be with Mama in 1969, to find her so badly battered that I couldn't even caress her. I remained in the States for a few years, keeping close to Mama, and doing nursing. This included work as a charge nurse in geriatrics at a local retirement home. Over a period of six months or so, my nurse's aides and I taught a lady with bilateral broken hip repairs to walk independently again, with the use of a walker. We also taught a man who had had a stroke to speak again. To me, this was just as exciting as working in an acute cardiac care unit. It just took longer to see the results.

SEVEN

KIBBUTZ LIFE VS. AMERICAN MATERIALISM

THROUGHOUT MUCH OF ISRAEL'S RECENT HISTORY, THE *KIBBUTZIM* AND *MOSHAVIM* HAVE BEEN THE BACKBONE OF THE NATION'S DEFENSE. These settlements suffer a great deal during crossfire with enemy states. They are settlements with communal sharing of all work and profits, while providing a private dwelling for each family. While in the kibbutz all property is commonly shared, and all profits are equally meted out, in the moshav each farm is owned by an individual family, with all members of the moshav working all of the farms together. In the kibbutz there is a common dining hall where everyone eats his or her meals. Each tiny family cabin has a few items of furniture, such as a small sofa, phonograph and records, and a personal library. Many kibbutznikim are prolific readers of classical Greek, Italian, and English literature, as well as classical Yiddish and Hebrew literature, all in the original languages.

Bearing in mind that many of the kibbutznikim who survived the Nazi Holocaust had originally been college professors, doctors, accountants, and other professionals, it is not difficult to envision the thirst that they have for knowledge, as well as an appreciation for good literature and the arts. In addition, each cabin is usually equipped with a hot plate for tea and a small refrigerator for snacks. The dining hall also serves a variety of religious and social functions on a communal basis, such as showing movies, at no charge, on a Saturday night.

Here festive and religious functions, such as the costume and comedy skit parties, with refreshments made on the kibbutz, are held on the Feast of Queen Esther, known as Purim, in the middle of March. This happiest of holidays is held to commemorate the triumph of the Jewish Queen Esther and her uncle, Mordecai, over the wicked Persian, Haman, who wished to have all the Jews of Persia put to death by King Ahashueros. However, out of his love for Esther, who fasted and asked that all of the Jews of Persia fast with her in asking pity of G-d, Ahashueros ordered Haman hanged from the gallows that he had erected to execute Mordecai, and the king passed an edict ordering that all Jews be protected. In remembrance of the event—and of the three-cornered hat worn by Haman—triangular pastries called *hamantashen*, filled with poppy seeds or apricot or prune jam, are baked and served with wine and fruit juice, along with other cakes and sweets. On the day before the partying begins and the sweets are served, the Book of Esther, called the Megillah, is read, and every time Haman's name is mentioned, all the congregants stamp their feet on the floor and the children sound metal noise-makers, that this wicked man's soul should not rest in peace. The reading of the Megillah takes about three hours or less.

The next day, on the Feast of Esther, the real fun begins, with everyone dressing up in the funniest costumes they can think of, and a carnival is held in the kibbutz, with the children being the chief performers. Children of the kibbutz compete in climbing up the flagpole, to see who can get to the highest point and then slide down. Young and old put burlap sacks over their feet to see who can jump the fastest to the finish line. At one of the celebrations I attended, a teenage woman and an elderly woman, both dressed in funny costumes, were given three-wheel toddler scooters to see who could drive the fastest to the finish line, with everyone rooting for the older woman, of course, and cheering her on, as she peddled with all her might. Some of the kibbutznikim dressed up as Arabs, others (in this free-thinking kibbutz) as Hassidim, some as Queen Esther and King Ahashueros, and some of the volunteers from foreign countries dressed as burlesque performers and floozies. My girlfriend, Leslie, dressed as a hippie, and I dressed as a fortune teller, with the result that many people asked me to tell their fortunes, so I had to think up some darned good stories fast—and I did. There were prizes of cakes and toys, of course, for the very best costumes, for both adults and children, and a great time was had by all.

Another happy time of the year is Chanukah, during the month of December. This holiday celebrates the triumph of the Jewish people, led by the Maccabee family, over the Assyrians (Greek invaders led by the infamous Antiochus Epiphanes). The Assyrians put many Jewish parents to death by hurling them from the rooftops, as punishment for practicing the Hebrew religious rite of circumcising their male children on the eighth day after birth. The Assyrians also desecrated the holy Temple in Jerusalem. When the Jews went to rekindle the oil lamp at the holy altar, there was only enough oil left for one day and one night, but miraculously the lamp burned for eight days and nights. For this reason we light a candle on the Chanukah candelabrum for each of the eight nights, with an extra one for G-d, while chanting the appropriate blessings. Also, a religious plastic or metal top with the Hebrew letters for N, G, H, and SH, representing "A great miracle was here," is given to each of the children, who have fun spinning it. In addition, special Chanukah donuts and potato *levivat* (like pancakes) are cooked for the occasion for everyone to partake of, and the chanting in Hebrew of Rock of Ages is done to commemorate the holiday. Also, parents, grandparents, and other older relatives of the children give them small money gifts called *Chanukah gelt* (Chanukah money).

In addition, on all the kibbutzim and moshavim, every Friday night (after candle blessing) and Saturday is an occasion for celebrating, as the Hebrew Sabbath is ushered in, and a party with cakes and wine or grape juice, called an *Oneg Shabbat,* is held for everybody. Dates, the candy of the desert, are also served. The Sabbath is a time, for all the parents and grandparents and their children to spend the whole day together, which they do not have a chance to do in the middle of the week. The grassy areas of the kibbutz and the flower gardens provide plenty of open space for the families to walk around and relax.

However, the crowning event in any kibbutz or moshav is a wedding, unique in its humbleness and its rustic flavor. The wedding hall is, of course, the main dining room, specially decorated with streamers and brightly colored decorations for the occasion. The dining hall also serves as the pre- and postnuptial reception hall, with an appropriate buffet dinner prepared for all. A rabbi, of course, officiates at the religious wedding ceremony, and all the family and friends of both bride and groom come here to offer congratulations. After the wedding ceremony comes the most important part of the celebration. The bride and groom, in all their finery, are taken on the back of a tractor for a drive all around the kibbutz or moshav grounds, as everyone calls out "Mazaltov" and throws confetti at the new couple. This is a unique part of kibbutz or moshav life; nowhere else in the world is a wedding celebrated in this way, in such a direct and humble fashion. At the end of the festivities, the newly married couple returns to what will be their own cabin for the rest of their lives.

Thus, though there are some who might think otherwise, life on the kibbutz and moshav is anything but boring, dull, and arduous. Moreover, each kibbutz and moshav must be provided with a live-in nurse and doctor, who are often accompanied by their families, together with a well-stocked infirmary, and emergency telephone and vehicle. There is also a central laundromat, sometimes with a dry cleaning facility, and a canteen store, where one can purchase items such as stamps, stationery, toiletries, cigarettes, sewing items, sugar, and tonic. Thus the kibbutz and moshav provide an almost totally self-sufficient unit in which its members live, including a schoolhouse for the children. Teachers for special courses, such as the advanced sciences and Arabic, are often brought in several days a week and are paid a special stipend.

Approximately half the country's produce comes from the two hundred eighty kibbutzim (comprising about five percent of Israel's population). In a small, struggling country this is an extremely important contribution. The kibbutz is an institution that originated in response to the desperate needs of groups of destitute, persecuted people who had survived the Nazi death camps. It has survived and flourished, together with the moshav, because it serves an important social and economic need. Both institutions provide everyone with a home and a job, full health care benefits, and familial care in the event of sudden illness or even death. While there is not much room for promotion or riches in this type of life, it provides a stability that many would otherwise not have. There is no such thing as apathy in the kibbutz or moshav. In the event of a catastrophe, everyone cares about everyone else.

One of the best examples of the application of the kibbutz and moshav spirit is in Tsahal, or the Israeli Armed Forces (IDF). The best leaders in all branches of the IDF, almost without exception, are kibbutz members. The sentiment of support for the good of the whole is very great here. Self-sacrifice to save one's fallen comrades is also very common. That is why we have such a high rate of casualties. When a soldier is wounded and falls on the front, he is never left behind; several fellow soldiers will rescue him. The officers set the standard by leading the others, so that we may lose officers also, in military skirmishes. Many tales have been told of unbelievable courage in Tsahal.

It is the courage of the Zwicka Gringolds of Israel that make us all proud to be Jewish. Zwicka Gringold, of whom some may already have heard, on furlough at the beginning of the Yom Kippur War, immediately went to the Golan Heights to help. For a day and a night Zwicka removed corpses from Israeli tanks, and driving them one at a time in hit-and-run fashion, managed to knock out enough of the Syrian tanks under General Jehani to allow time for Israeli reinforcements to relieve him. Zwicka was later awarded the Order of Courage, Israel's highest honor. There are thousands of other soldiers like Zwicka in Israel.

In addition to the spirit of self-sacrifice in the kibbutz, life in it demands a rigorous schedule. In my kibbutz life, it was up at 3:30 a.m. to get washed and dressed and be driven by truck out to the fields by 4:00 a.m., have some tea and bread with jam, and start picking peaches, grapefruits, and oranges till 8:00 a.m. Then we were served a hearty breakfast of scrambled eggs with tomatoes and onions, plus cucumbers, bread with margarine, and coffee. After that it was back to the fields to continue work till noon. Next we had lunch in the communal dining hall, rested a little, and went to the ulpan classes.

There is a reason for this schedule in the Middle East. During summer the heat can sometimes reach over a hundred degrees Fahrenheit by noon (in the Sinai and Judean deserts, up to a hundred and twenty degrees in the sun, and a hundred and ten in the shade), making work of any sort impossible. Thus the workday in the Middle East is set up in halves: 8:00 a.m. to 1:00 p.m., break, and then 4:00 p.m. to 7:00 p.m. There is a period of summer called *chamsin* (fifty, in Arabic), meaning fifty days of intense, broiling heat. During these times, work output is at a minimum.

My next and last kibbutz experience was at Kibbutz HaMaapil (whose name refers to the original, illegal immigrants into what was then Palestine under the British mandate in the late 1940's), near Hadera, in central Israel. I had quite a number of learning experiences there. For one thing, as I mentioned earlier, kibbutz workers left for the fields at 4:00 a.m., when it was still quite dark. Israel has a number of venomous, as well as non-venomous, snakes and other reptiles in its forests, and one of nature's ways of protecting these creatures is by coloration that resembles the tree leaves and branches. Thus sometimes it was too late to recognize such a creature in the branches of a fruit tree till we were upon it. Some of the men carried knives for that reason, and one morning, as we were all up in the trees a little after 4:00 a.m., one of the men gave a grunt as he cut a pit viper behind the head, just as the snake was about to strike. It was a bit unpleasant, but there was no malice in the act; as Rudyard Kipling might have said, "This is the law of the jungle." These incidents did not happen very often, though, and kibbutznikim would strike an animal only in self-defense. The lives of animals were never taken in a wanton manner in the kibbutz or moshav.

There was another time when, not being very graceful on ladders, I let out a scream as I began to topple from the tree. Bless the souls of two quick-acting kibbutz men, one of whom grabbed the ladder while the other broke my fall and caught me. I was never so grateful to anyone.

While working in the fields I got to know Shika, a very special man of relatively short stature and slim build, with fair features and piercingly intense blue eyes. Shika had been a college professor in Poland till the advent of Hitler, and could converse intelligently in Hebrew, Yiddish, Polish, and English. His whole family had been put to death at the Auschwitz concentration camp. Only he had survived, with the tattooed numbers still on his forearm, like most of the other kibbuznikim, as nearly all were death camp survivors.

He was not tolerant of any anti-Israel comments that were made occasionally by foreign volunteers on the kibbutz, and responded directly with facts about inhuman acts performed on Jews in Arab nations, such as Iraq. He defended his people and his land completely, for which I respected him very much. Moreover, though he had gone through a living hell, and been reduced from being a professor to laboring as a fruit picker, Shika showed me an amazing degree of friendliness and fatherly helpfulness, which he also showed to other newcomers. He reserved his greatest warmth, though, for those of us who expected to stay in the land and help build it, as he and the other death camp survivors had done. It is amazing what a capacity for warmth the human soul can hold.

Nissim was our supervisor of volunteers. Stocky, of average height, with grayish black hair combed straight back, Nissim had a serious appearance and manner, but he could be very friendly on occasion. Though he demanded a good output of work from us, along with everyone else, he was also very considerate. When he saw that I didn't mind doing extra overtime work during sudden military emergencies, which left few behind to do the kitchen work, Nissim rewarded me by letting me have an old wooden cabin all to myself. That was a luxury.

We volunteers didn't know the half of it as far as stress was concerned. Every night several kibbutz members, men and women, would have to stand guard with their rifles ready for instant action, in the event of terrorist infiltrators in the forest. Their drawn, ashen looks in the morning told the story of their physical and emotional strain, of having had to watch, in the pitch darkness, the movement of anything suspicious, in the trees and shrubbery, for eight hours solid. What a pampered upbringing we American youngsters have had, by comparison.

I was overwhelmingly impressed by the mutual caring and spontaneous involvement by kibbutz members in gathering crops, cleaning filth from chicken coops, and helping fellow members in times of distress. A genuine feeling of oneness became part of me as fellow kibbutznik, Rina, and I peeled eggplants and scrubbed the kibbutz kitchen together. If one kibbutz member fell ill or met with misfortune, everyone rallied to help him or her and their family. There was the time when fellow kibbutz member Tzvi took seriously ill and required open-heart surgery. A number of kibbutz men immediately rushed to Tel HaShomer Hospital to give him blood, while the women comforted his wife and children. When he died, the whole kibbutz had a mourning ceremony and supported the family. In the kibbutz the old and the sick are not put out to pasture. They remain and are cared for in the kibbutz. I greatly admire this interdependency and caring. These are the same principles that the late Anwar El-Sadat wrote of in his autobiography, describing the participation of the villagers to help each farmer irrigate his field till all had been irrigated in his native village of Abul-Kum.[1]

This is where the real "Women's Libbers" came from, wives and daughters who tilled fields, forked up horse manure, and drained malarial swamps side by side with their menfolk, in addition to cooking, baking, washing, and sewing—sometimes even without an oven run on gas or piped-in running water—without complaining about it.

In contrast to the materialistic society in urban United States (or to a lesser extent in Israel today), which values its color television sets, stereos, and cars, the real people of accomplishment were and are those Israeli pioneers who did not mind soiling their hands and who defended their land from marauders. In this vein, at one point in the early 1950's, when some of my family first immigrated to Israel from Romania, on Passover they ate lima beans (which, as legumes, are forbidden on Passover) together with onions and potatoes, because there was little else to eat.

Let none of us in the United States complain about a lack of, or inadequate, air conditioning at work in summer. In Israel and most of the Middle East during the 1960's there were not even fans for the weary laborers, many of whom toiled in steaming, mosquito-infested swamps. Today, for that matter, many health care and work facilities in the Middle East still have fans, not air conditioners. It would be too costly and use up too much electricity. However, some of the more sophisticated buildings, including hospitals and hotels, now have air conditioning.

All of this mutual participation and caring in the Israeli kibbutz, contrasted with American materialism, points to the stark difference between Israel and the United States in their conception of the relationship between the individual and the community. In the United States, under the free enterprise system, people are conditioned and encouraged to "pull themselves up by their own bootstraps" and compete to whatever extent they can in school, business, play, and work. Though I am sure it was not the intention of our Founding Fathers (who wrote the Constitution), it is often done at the expense of and without sensitivity to the feelings and welfare of those who are deprived. Concern for the self, and individual initiative, are stressed.

A number of other local residents and I were very much chagrined when our druggist was run out of business (after serving the community for over thirty-five years) by a CVS store opening in a nearby.mall. The same thing happened when a new food chain moved into the area, close to an old First National store that had given the community excellent service for many years, so that the First National store soon closed. Had the government stepped in (as is done in some socialist countries) to order each of the new stores to locate at a sufficient distance from those already in operation, no harm would have been done to the original stores.

Likewise, a recent Carnegie Institute study reported that the idea of getting ahead in college by any means has fostered cramming for exams, cheating, and some students paying other people to write their term papers. In addition, according to the study, the meaningfulness of college students being prepared to contribute to the community after graduation has been forgotten, to a large extent. It has been replaced by the idea of getting college over in order to get a high-paying job, rather than getting an education for its own sake. Though some of these ideas had crept into the system when I was still in college, it was not as widespread as it is now.

By contrast, it is not only in the kibbutz and the moshav in Israel that mutual caring is to be found, but also in Israeli society in general. The poorest families pitch in to celebrate a wedding or a circumcision; likewise, when a death occurs in a family, most friends and neighbors, as well as relatives, come to offer respect and bring food to the bereaved family. This mutual caring is indispensable.

It is a special quality that Americans once had, but no longer seem to possess very much. I can remember that quality in Chelsea forty-five years ago, when neighbors on a city block still cared. When a housewife fell seriously ill, one neighbor would come to wash the floors, and another would feed the children, gratis. Those were the days when Jewish charities saw to it that every poor Jewish family received a check and/or grocery order for Passover, as well as at other times of the year.

Now many underprivileged Jewish families do without, while substantial funds are channeled to such causes as lettuce, grapes, and other minority group causes. The ethics of Judaism teaches helping the needy of all races and creeds, but charity begins at home, and charity to fellow Jews should come first. It has especially come to be the project of some of the Reformed Jews to espouse non-Jewish causes, sometimes even to the point of (however inadvertently) desecration of Judaism. A certain local congregation, which we shall call T.M.T., saw fit twenty years ago to celebrate a Passover seder in a Christian church. They could just as easily have invited the church members to the synagogue or to a private Jewish home for the seder. Holding Jewish holy observances in an edifice under the sign of the Cross constitutes a sacrilege.

Furthermore, true Jewish education, which is at the core of Judaism, can be fostered only in an Orthodox environment, where all the basic books of Judaism, such as *Humash* and *Talmud* (teaching), are taught in Hebrew, not English or another language. Of course, we should be aware of the correct translation in our native language also, but the basics must be taught in Hebrew. Certain Hebrew expressions lose their meaning upon translation. This is why it is so urgent that the Orthodox Yeshivot (schools) be supported in every Jewish community in the United States, as well as abroad.

This view seems to be anathema to some Jewish savants of Greater Boston, who have stated publicly that the education and religious beliefs of the Jews of America should not be dictated by either Christianity or Orthodox Judaism. Perhaps these people would prefer to see the American Jewish culture fade out via assimilation. We cannot afford to overlook such statements, especially at a time when all Jews should band together in the face of international and local anti-Semitism (in the form of attacks on Jews, synagogue desecrations, and painting of swastikas on Jewish homes in the past five decades). The advocacy of Orthodox Jewish education is no more a threat to American civil liberties than the pledge of allegiance to the flag.

EIGHT

JEWS AND PALESTINIANS: A DILEMMA

In the course of my public health nursing in Tsvat, I was exposed to working with both Jews and Palestinians in Tsvat and in the neighboring Arab and Druze villages. From the Jewish mothers, and from the Arab and Druze mothers of Magdal Shams, I constantly heard, "We want peace. We want our children to live to bury us, not for us to bury them. Otherwise, let us die now, so we will not live to see another child die in battle." The Druzim are a group of Arabs, followers of Ishmael Ad-Darazhi, whose religion requires, unlike the Muslim faith, that they must live near a well or water hole in order to maintain daily personal cleanliness. In the Muslim faith it is permitted to symbolically practice one's ablutions five times a day, if people are living in a desert area far away from a well or bathing place.

When I was among the Druzim, I observed that every dirt floor was swept clean, and though all the women wore heavy, black dresses with white head cloths covering them almost completely, they and their children were all well-groomed and spotlessly clean. I could not detect even a slight body odor on them. They and their homes were all in perfect order. Some Druzim who decided to open up to me admitted that though their previous Syrian rulers had been cruel to them on occasion, they still preferred to be under Arab rather than Israeli domination. They said that after all, they were an Arab people who belonged among Arabs, rather than Israelis. Magdal Shams, by the way, happens to be located exactly at the juncture of the Syrian-Israeli border, which puts the Druzim in a very precarious situation, being constantly exposed to crossfire between the two nations. I learned much from my limited exposure to the Druze culture and community.

Again, in the course of my public health nursing I found the Palestinian mothers very affable as I blundered through my broken Arabic, trying to treat my patients. This is in contrast to the incorrect picture drawn by many Westerners of all Arabs as being conniving, bloodthirsty people. The people with whom I dealt were anything but that.

Perhaps the need of a permanent peace, plus the agonizing losses of war, were best summed up in the late Anwar El-Sadat's autobiography:

> I lost my younger brother, who was like a son to me, five minutes after the start of the October War. I have seen the victims of that war—young people destined to spend the rest of their lives in wheelchairs. I have seen similar cases in Israel and felt equally sad. One cannot help being deeply moved by the sight of the war victims, whoever and wherever they may be, and it was this spirit that helped me to achieve the two targets of my visit to Jerusalem.[1]

Though he was known as a somewhat autocratic leader in Egypt, let us not forget that President Anwar El-Sadat did make important changes in the health clinics and penal system in his country. Also, he was the first Arab national leader in the history of the Middle East to come forward with a proposal for peace with Israel. To quote his quote of the Koran: "We offered responsibility to the Earth, the Heavens, and the Mountains, but they declined to bear it and felt unequal to it. Man bears it."[2]

A number of Arab families were forced off their land in 1948, and this must be rectified by adequate measures—return of land and homes, or monetary compensation. However, most Arabs left of their own volition, having been promised by the Mufti of Jerusalem and others of their leaders that they were leaving only temporarily and would all return to Palestine after the Jews were driven out. Also, there were murders and pillaging of Jewish settlements by hostile Arabs, with no provocation whatever.

Of the so-called "displaced Palestinian refugees," none have been welcomed to live among their fellow Arab nations. Well over a billion dollars has been spent by the United Nations to maintain these people in their camps, with over half the bill being footed by the United States. Most of the Palestinians who left Israel in the 1948 War of Independence did not leave any great deal of wealth behind them. This was in sharp contrast to the Jews who left Arab countries, such as Iraq, Morocco, and Yemen, in many instances through no choice of their own. During that period they were forced to abandon homes, land, businesses, and a great deal of sacred property and were welcomed by their fellow Jews in the new state of Israel. These Sephardi Jews have since contributed greatly to the spiritual, industrial, and economic growth of Israel. On the contrary, in the fifty years that have elapsed, the Arab states have kept their "guest" Palestinians on the international dole, and in a constant, "educational" process of induction into such terrorist groups as the Palestinian Liberation Organization and the Islamic Hezbollah.

Also on the Palestinian-Jewish problem, we must remember that the Jews who survived the Holocaust wanted to go to Israel, and were not welcomed by any other nations except Denmark, Sweden, and the nation now called the People's Republic of China. (This is a good time to make note of those few nations who truly befriended the Jews in their darkest hour.) Since then, as a result of the 1948 war, the United Nations decided for partition, and Israel had the borders it did till the 1967 War, when Israel gained control of Jerusalem and the West Bank and Gaza.

Many outsiders have had harsh comments to make about the Israeli military administering the West Bank and Gaza. Here is where the severe turmoil begins. The territories had to be administered, and law and order kept, especially in an area that was known to harbor many PLO terrorists. I personally can attest to the political situation from my experiences on the West Bank. As a nurse I became acquainted with a number of dignified Palestinian Arabs and foreign nationals working in medical-associated professions. They were all very fine people, dedicated to serving humanity. I would never divulge their identities, lest they be made to pay for it with their lives, at the hands of the *intifada* people. The latter consist of a large number of very impressionable young men, whose *kaffiyeh*-covered faces, together with swords and axes, give them a symbolic "macho" status, as they beat, mutilate, and murder any fellow Arabs who associate with or work for Israelis. The unpardonable attack in February 1994 on a Jewish vehicle passing through Gaza, where a pregnant Israeli woman was shot in the abdomen and the head, killing her, and leaving her husband and child alive is one of the worst examples of Arab barbarism and cannot be allowed to pass with impunity.

I am certain that this was among the incidents that drove Dr. Baruch Goldstein to open fire on a group of Muslims at prayer at a mosque in Hebron on February 25, 1994, killing over forty people and wounding many others. I can understand the frustration, though I certainly cannot condone this act. Since and before the Rabin-Arafat peace talks initiated on the White House lawn in September of 1993, militant Palestinians have been picking off Jew after Jew to murder wantonly. The Israeli military cannot acquiesce to this murdering of innocent Jews. However, the massacre in the mosque did not right a wrong either. Only one unstable man was responsible for the killings at the mosque, and this does not justify condemning all Jewish settlers on the West Bank. For the time being, the Israeli military needs to supervise the West Bank and, until recently, Gaza. It is a situation that cannot go on perpetually, though. It costs Israeli Defense a very high price daily in military equipment, hostilities, and Jewish lives.

No one ever objected when the Turks or the British ruled over what was then called Palestine (named for the ancient Philistines who originally lived there). It was only when the Hebrew nation came into being in 1948 that the other nations of this world suddenly became displeased that there should be a Zionist state. The United Nations grudgingly voted for partition, for a small Jewish state and a separate, small Palestinian state under Jordanian rule. Since and including 1948, Israel has had to fight for its existence four times, at an extremely high cost of human lives, let alone military equipment.

Not one of those wars did Israel bring on itself. It was being attacked and had to defend itself. When any other nation has emerged victorious and captured territory, no one has raised an eyebrow. However, when in 1967 Israel placed the West Bank and Gaza under Israeli military rule, great cries arose, including those from the United Nations, some of whose members have had the gall to equate Zionism with racism. Though the system of Israeli rule has had its flaws, it has been a much more beneficent and productive rule than under Jordan. Under Israeli rule six universities have been established on the West Bank and five Arab newspapers exist. Farming, health clinics, roads, and electric power have improved tremendously.

In a very eloquent, though distorted, fashion, NBC television, on July 1, 1987, broadcast a program entitled "Twenty Years Later—A Dream Is Dying." In it NBC suggested that due to brutal oppression by the Israelis, Palestinians were responding with violence. This is grossly untrue. As I traveled through the West Bank, I found it very upsetting to hear a ten-year-old Arab boy exclaiming, "I want to grow up to be like Yassir Arafat. I want to kill Jews and make Palestine ours again." (My friend Laura interpreted that for me.)

In contrast, I have been very impressed by the remarkable restraint used by most Israeli soldiers in patrolling the West Bank towns of Nablus, Hebron, and Jericho. It sometimes requires great restraint on the part of the Israelis when groups of Palestinian school children (mostly teenagers) jeer in dirty language and throw rocks at them, as they pass by on patrol. Most of the time the soldiers, when pelted with rocks, shout for the crowd to disperse, and fire their rifles into the air. However, when soldiers are being hit and badly hurt by rocks and/or hand grenades that adults and some children are taught to throw at them, they sometimes have to shoot back.

Martin Gallanter, in a 1988 article for the *Boston Jewish Times*, quotes comments by some young Jewish soldiers that vividly express their perspective. One named Danny stated: "It goes on all day and all night. We sleep with our weapons and our gear, ready to be called in case we are needed in the village. We get no rest—under constant pressure and then one of us makes a mistake and it becomes an international incident." Another young soldier said, "And what if we were not there? Who would protect the innocent people, the ones who don't throw stones, who want only to live in peace? Would the PLO protect them?" One last pithy comment was made by another soldier: "We know that the Jews overseas are upset. Tell them for us that we like doing this even less than they like watching it on TV."[3]

The journalists already referred to overlook the existence in Israel of the Council for Peace and Security, formed by a number of Israel Defense Force reserve generals and other officers who had been trying to alter the political situation in Gaza and the West Bank and to revamp Israel's policy there. These officers have had an effective voice in Yossi Sarid, a former Knesset (Israeli Parliament) member, who quoted the number of Palestinians killed and wounded since the inception of the *intifada,* or uprising, in late 1987. Sarid persuaded many of the Knesset and former Defense Minister Yitzhak Rabin to have a dialogue with "all sectors in the administered territories." Major General Shlomo Gazit of the Council for Peace and Security has stated that coexistence between Israelis and Palestinians must be directed by a new policy that advocates neither the expulsions of Palestinians nor Israel's giving up the territories. Moderation has been the consistently advocated policy of the Council.[4]

Several years ago, General Amram Mitzna, then commander of the West Bank, was quoted as having said, "Everyone in Israel has an opinion of what to do. The have opinions, with none of the responsibility. Many of them don't understand the limitations. You can't just go around and kill and beat people just because they throw a stone." General Mitzna even braved the criticism of the right wing Likud faction for ordering the arrest of four soldiers and their officer for beating two Palestinian demonstrators. Also, General Mitzna stated to foreign journalists that the beating of Palestinians "is our problem now, not the problem of the media and not the problem of the people outside of the forces to deal with."[5] In a truly democratic society such as exists in Israel, men like General Mitzna are allowed to speak out against what they feel is unjust.

Also, the conscientious people of the world seemed to have had their attention directed elsewhere when in 1983, forewarned that something of this nature could happen, Indian Prime Minister Indira Gandhi took no precautions, and a group of Hindu fanatics massacred several hundred Muslims. Only brief international mention was made of this, yet the media have for several years continued to heap blame on Israel for the massacre of Palestinians in two refugee camps by Lebanese Christian militia. There seems to be something very distorted in these media presentations.

Recently the American news media has seen fit to take issue with Israel's restricting certain Arab-Americans and African-Americans from visiting their families on the West Bank and elsewhere. The security division of Israel knows what it is doing when it restricts potentially subversive visitors to the country.

In addition, Israel owes no apology when it restricts certain anti-Semitic African-Americans who are affiliated with the self-styled "Black Jews" of Dimona, from entering the country as tourists. The only regret we need have here is that this group of virulent anti-Semites were allowed to settle when they first came to Israel in 1973 under the leadership of the self-titled Ben Ami Carter. He had stated, together with his group, that because he felt American Jews were to blame for the ills that had befallen African-Americans, that gave them the right to assume their own idea of a "Black Jewish" religion, and for them to take what was due them.[6]

The strong moral and financial support of American Jews helped create the National Association for the Advancement of Colored People. It was out of genuine concern for people who were being treated unjustly that a Jew such as Sol Hurok, the great impresario, supported Marian Anderson in 1939, en route to her becoming one of the greatest contralto singers in the world. Attorney Felix Cohen also supported Miss Anderson's endeavors, in the face of bitter opposition from the Daughters of the American Revolution, who refused to allow Miss Anderson to appear in Constitution Hall in Washington, D.C.[7]

It was other Jews of conviction, such as the late Rabbi Henry Cohen of Galveston, Texas, working with Father Kirwin, who both dared to oppose the Ku Klux Klan and led the whole community in preventing the Klan from parading down Market Street, a main street of Galveston. These events took place long before the civil rights marches of the 1960's; they occurred in the early 1900's.[8]

It was Jews named Andrew Goodman and Michael Schwerner who, together with James Cheney, were found brutally murdered on August 4, 1964, in their attempt to establish equal rights for African-Americans in Philadelphia, Mississippi.

All these are but a few examples of American Jews who gave all they could, in some cases their lives, for the betterment of African-Americans. There have been many more such examples. Thus, neither the Jews of

America nor the Jews of Israel should need to suffer for what others have inflicted on African-Americans or other minority groups.

What the Jews of America and of Israel do need to concern themselves with are the sometimes negative impressions given international journalists by the Orthodox Jewish Gush Emunim (Block of Believers) group, who feel that all of Israel, including the West Bank, belongs exclusively to Jews. They are angry that, once apprehended, Arabs such as Abu Nidal, who murder Jews, are given jail sentences, rather than being executed. In such cases also, the house of the terrorist is sometimes blown up. I do not dispute the fact that the Old Testament states that G-d gave the Hebrew people all of the land of Israel, including the areas currently known as Judea and Samaria. In areas that are not populated by Arabs, Israeli Jews should be free to erect settlements, such as Kiryat Arba, and Beitar on the West Bank. We are a people who have one small place on the face of the earth to inhabit, and no one has the right to deny us that.

Still we must respect Palestinians of integrity, such as Mohammed Milhelm, one of the original founders of the Peace Now movement, who has been deported for political connections with the late Yassir Arafat. Out of antagonism stemming from ill treatment by Israeli authorities, I believe that Mr. Milhelm turned to Arafat, but certainly not because he is a treasonable man. Like other Arab moderates who did not really like Arafat but supported him because he embodied the idea of a Palestinian homeland, Mr. Milhelm had consorted with Arafat to a limited extent. We must communicate with and support men like Mohammed Milhelm, who risk their lives for peace.

The Peace Now movement was initiated by Mordecai Bar-On and Mohammed Milhelm, and it advocates the return of some of the conquered lands by Israel to achieve peace with the Arab states. The Gush Emunim people resent it that the NBC producers failed to note that only Israel, and not one Arab state, has such a pro-peace movement, on a national level. Peace may come someday between Arabs and Jews, although I believe it will not come until the coming of the Messiah (according to Jewish prophecy). Delusional concepts of peace in the Middle East, such as those pursued by former Secretary of State Warren Christopher, will not determine when peace will come. Furthermore, the ancient Arab belief in blood vendettas will never give way to sound reasoning. If those energies could be rerouted into efforts for education, improved health care for all, and water purification, then there could be progress.

To this end there have been a number of Palestinian Arabs who have worked valiantly for peace, such as Yussaf Al-Khatib, head of the Village Association of Ramallah. Al-Khatib had been working on a peace mission with the Israelis when in November 1981 the Palestinian Liberation Organization, which later took responsibility for the murders, killed him and his son, Khazem, en route to Ramallah. Similarly, a man who headed the Hebron Hills Village Association, Moustapha Doudin, was threatened by the PLO. He had spoken out against violence between Arabs, in particular referring to the 1937 riots and killings among Arabs. Many other, honorable Palestinians have spoken out for peace, and have been silenced by the late Yassir Arafat, George Habash, and their cohorts. Until recently these men have refused to recognize the existence of the State of Israel (though Arafat eventually recognized Israel). Other terrorists, in conjunction with Hezbollah and with Syrian backing, still continue their attacks against Israel and her people.[9]

If the late King Hussein of Jordan had seen fit to participate in negotiations with Israel after 1985 about setting up a Palestinian state under Jordanian aegis, with the leadership coming from well-qualified West Bank Arabs, this confrontation might never have happened. Also, whenever Israel has broached closing down and/or resettling a Palestinian refugee camp for health or other reasons, the United Nations has prevented it, insisting that the refugee camps remain as they are, in the West Bank and Gaza. Under these circumstances, it has been difficult for Israel to fulfill the Camp David Accord.

American journalists have condemned the Israeli army's using tear gas, rubber bullets, and then live ammunition on crowds of stone- and bottle-throwing Arab youths. They failed to make note of the Israeli who was stoned in Gaza several years ago, and who was in critical condition as a result of the injuries inflicted. Let no one underestimate the harm that can be done by throwing rocks and bottles, in particular Molotov cocktails (gasoline-soaked rags stuffed into bottles, ignited, and then thrown at someone), which have an extremely explosive, incendiary effect.

Where is the outcry from American citizens against Sheik Omar Abdel Rahman and his evil cohorts, who caused the bombing of the World

Trade Center in New York in February 1993, killing at least six people and wounding hundreds more? There was a world outcry in response to Osama bin Laden's masterminding and then carrying out the bombing of the World Trade Center, with approximately three thousand persons murdered and thousands more injured on September 11, 2001. These were carefully planned and executed plots by extremist Arab Hezbollah and Al Qaeda terrorists to inflict devastation, death, and suffering on innocent Americans. Also, what about the Hamas suicide explosion of a bus filled with Orthodox Israeli families, mostly children, on August 19, 2003, in Jerusalem, killing over twenty and injuring over a hundred?

As for past terrorist attacks, I can speak on this subject from my involvement as a medical volunteer in caring for victims of a PLO bombing, and later as a nurse in caring for both Jews and Arabs wounded in the Yom Kippur War. The first such attack I saw was in 1968 when the PLO planted a car bomb containing two hundred pounds of dynamite with a timer device at the rear of the Mahane Yehuda shuk, near a Jewish hairdresser's salon. The explosive was placed there, with diabolic intent, near huge vats of olive oil and large quantities of flammable textiles. It was set to go off at mid-morning on a Friday, the one time when the shuk is filled with mostly women, children, and old people who shop to prepare for the Hebrew Sabbath. Fate must have been with me, as I was standing only a few yards from the car bomb a while earlier, when my conscience told me to leave, so as not to be late for the ulpan class. An hour later, the grim announcement of the explosion was made to us at Ulpan Etzion, and I volunteered, together with a number of other medical people, to help.

Though we arrived on the scene after the fact, the horrorible scene was beyond belief. Blood and pieces of human bodies were everywhere. A twelve-year-old Arab boy with third-degree burns gasped his last breath as the flesh fell off his bones. An old man groaned in agony with six compound fractures protruding through the flesh of his legs. The hairdresser's assistant was killed instantly, and the hairdresser himself screamed in pain, with chunks of flesh hanging off his face, arms, and chest. This mentions only a few. The smell of burning flesh permeated the whole area. Much to our shame, most of us did nothing to help the victims, but stood there and vomited. Fortunately, the emergency response teams from Shaare Zedek Hospital set up triage and rescue at once, quickly evacuating the wounded to their own and other hospitals, in coordination with Red Star of David rescue squads.

There was another such terrorist attack that I did not witness, but which stands out from among the rest as the worst: the attack at Maalot in northern Israel in 1974. There PLO terrorists hurled screaming Jewish children from the school rooftop to dash their brains out against the cement pavement below, as their horrified parents watched, helpless. It makes my blood boil to think of people who cruelly, premeditatedly take the lives of innocent children. In response to these terrorist attacks, of course the IDF struck back at terrorist bases in Lebanon. At once there was an uproar among the international media about Israel's invading another nation and causing casualties.

All these upright people who rushed to complain about Israeli soldiers beating two Arab terrorists overlooked the fact that the terrorists had murdered a bus full of Israeli civilians. It seems more politically advantageous to be pro-Arab terrorist than pro-Jewish soldiers. These hypocritical people who judge Jewish soldiers and not Arab terrorists have a very warped sense of humanity and justice.

When the media talk about Israeli incursions into Arab lands in retaliation for terrorist attacks, to me this reinforces the great importance of Israel's having secure borders. For this reason the most ardent supporters of Peace Now will not consider returning Jerusalem or the Golan Heights, from among the territories acquired during the 1967 War. Jerusalem embodies the heart of Judaism, and all other faiths are given respect within its boundaries. As for the Golan Heights, not only remembering the horrific bloodshed that the Israelis suffered from the Syrians during the Yom Kippur War, but also the vicious shelling that border settlements suffered from Syria, Israel must not relinquish this vulnerable point in its defense again. Israel is always open to negotiations, but not to compromising its defense and therefore its survival.

Quite often when foreigners hear of terrorist attacks on Israelis, they ask how we can possibly live in such a state of constant fear. It is true that terrorist attacks do occur in Israel (as well as in many other nations of the world lately). However, nowhere else in the world do women going to a concert at night, with pocketbooks on their arms, feel more secure than in

Israel. In all of Israel's cities, especially in potential trouble areas, security forces are posted at frequent intervals throughout the community, both in uniform and in plain clothes. I have never felt so secure as I did in my three years in Israel, both before and after my marriage. My friends and family and I went out visiting or to the theater, sometimes late at night, and went home by public transportation. In all my years in the United States I have not yet experienced the feeling of security that I did in Israel. In Israel the cities and towns, as well as villages and borders, are always well defended.

The Palestinian refugee problem has been and continues to be a convenient political platform, not only for the Arab states, but also for countries with anti-Jewish leanings, from which to heap disparagement on Israel and Jewish people. Most European countries, with the exception of England, have not condemned terrorists. Germany, however, convicted Hezbollah's Mohammed Ali Hamadi when, in the name of the Palestinian cause, he brutally executed innocent civilians in transit on TWA Flight 847 on June 14, 1985. A solution to the West Bank refugee problems must be found, but under the auspices of the Israeli government and local competent Arab leaders, not the PLO or any other Jacobin-mob-type group of uncontrolled fanatics.

NINE

THE YOM KIPPUR WAR

In October of 1973 came the shock of the Yom Kippur War. I felt that my place was with my people, so I packed my possessions, and after consulting with my friends and family and the Israeli consulate, I flew to Israel. All was in chaos there. A pall of gloom hung over everyone. The soldiers of the Seventh Armored Brigade had suffered the bloodiest losses, as the Syrians sent more tanks onto the Golan Heights than the Germans had against the Russians in the Second World War. These were in addition to the losses at Sinai, the Suez Canal, and elsewhere. Some families were sitting on the floor in mourning for two sons killed on different fronts. The Ministry of Defense sees to the material needs of every family that loses a husband, son, or daughter in defense of the country, indefinitely. However, this is small consolation to a young wife with three or four children who has to bury her husband.

Save for those who have lost relatives in the World Wars, Vietnam, or Iraq, we in American can barely begin to fathom the tragic impact of the war on Israelis, as well as on other countries. Israel is a small country, where every family feels the loss of a child as if it were their own. Most of the immigrants to Israel have come from terrible persecutions in places such as Iraq, Syria, Ethiopia, and Nazi Germany during the Second World War. They have come back to their homeland, for their children to have a homeland. For an Israeli, fighting for Israel means not only defending home and family, but also defending the Jewish people.

I was sent to the northern front first, to a station on the Lebanese-Syrian frontier, where I got to observe what a living hell was really like. The station included medical facilities for emergency war use and a landing pad for medi-choppers. These were situated in a huge open space enclosed by a high barbed wire and electrically charged fence. The area is near Mount Hermon, Israel's highest peak, where even in summer there is sometimes snow. The howling, bitter wind that hit the entire area, in combination with hailstones, cut through the strongest people and beasts. There was no shelter whatever there, not even a single tree to shield us from the wind and rain as we made our way from medical tents to surgical units.

On my first day at this station I encountered in one of the medical tents a soldier who had been hit in the abdomen by a shell, which caused his intestines to eviscerate. He was shouting in severe pain, and I rushed to undertake his care. Any qualified medical person knows that no attempt should be made to immediately reinsert the intestines into the abdomen. Since his respirations were above the critical rate of sixteen per minute, I covered the area with a sterile saline cloth and administered a quarter-grain of morphine. Another nurse, Bracha, administered intravenous normal saline to prevent dehydration.

Next, I turned my attention to one of the medics, Yossi, who had been hit in the right eye by a shell fragment. He refused to be relieved of his duty though, and insisted on going about checking the other patients' blood pressure. Meantime, an Israeli X-ray technician, Uram (who told me just what he thought of me as an American practitioner), guided me through setting a soldier's fractured left arm, successfully. Then we prepared the eviscerated soldier, the soldier with a fracture, and Yossi (who agreed only grudgingly) to be airlifted by medi-chopper to Tel HaShomer Hospital. We were later told that all three survived and that Yossi's eye had been saved. The eviscerated soldier had a partial colectomy and later recovered.

It was not uncommon in this medical triage crisis for nurses and medics to be given tasks such as minor surgery, setting fractures, and treating mild eviscerations while the few doctors and surgeons treated more urgent and complex cases—soldiers who had been shot in the neck, hit by mortars in the chest or abdomen, had limbs shot off, or had massive abdominal eviscerations. My colleague Bracha demonstrated the kind of bravery that was not unusual in this setting when she was suddenly called to a soldier who had been hit in the throat by a shell and was fighting to breathe. She seized a scalpel, palpated for the third cricoid cartilage, plunged the scalpel in below it, and inserted an airway into the bloody opening. We were running out of sterile equipment, so Bracha secured the airway with an unsterile length of gauze, tying it to one side. Then the soldier began to breathe, and she injected a quarter-grain of morphine into his arm. She had saved his life. Had I been called upon to perform that procedure, I would not have had the nerve to do it.

I was distracted by horrific screaming and was summoned by medic Eli to Dr. Kazlov's tent. He stood over a severely eviscerated soldier who had been hit by a mortar in the abdomen. Blood poured from the wound. Although the doctor had already given the soldier two doses of morphine, he instructed me to inject him with another grain of morphine. I followed his instruction and then held the soldier's hand in mine to let him know that another human being cared. Dr. Kazlov and I both stood over him for ten minutes more until he was out of his misery. As I stood there, I thought, "There is one thing worse than cancer, and that is war."

The next casualty I dealt with was a soldier who had been hit in the chest by shrapnel and was bleeding badly. In disaster medicine we learn never to probe for shrapnel, in case we should accidentally sever a large blood vessel or a nerve. I immediately applied a heavy pressure dressing to the wound and taped it onto him. His breathing rate was sixteen respirations per minute, so I administered a quarter grain of morphine. Only a few days earlier we had run out of all morphine and dry sterile dressing sets, as well as sterile suture sets, but, thank G-d, the Americans had sent us enough replacement dressing and suture sets, needles and syringes filled with Demerol, and a goodly number of vials of Novocaine and Xylocaine. Twenty minutes later the soldier was still shouting in pain, so I asked Eli, the medic, to help me gently pull off his pants and turn him, so that I could inject him in the left buttock with a hundred milligrams of Demerol. After another twenty minutes, his pain had been relieved.

Shortly thereafter, Dr. Kazlov called for Bracha and me to help him with a soldier who had received one of the worst kinds of wound, a compound fracture of the left leg. (In a compound fracture the bone splits in two and pierces the flesh and skin.) Very gingerly we placed two full-length wooden leg splints, one below the leg and one above, and wrapped them with gauze to completely immobilize the limb. Then, as the patient's respirations were sixteen, Bracha injected the other leg in the thigh with a hundred milligrams of Demerol plus, at Dr. Kazlov's order, twenty-five milligrams of Phenergan to enhance the pain relief.

Finally we got the patients stable enough that they could eat some hummus with tahina and pita bread with two cups of tea and some egg salad. As we patiently waited for the next medi-choppers to arrive, Dr. Kazlov decided that groups of three of us should take three-hour naps while the rest monitored the patients. After the three hours, the other staff switched with us to sleep while we monitored the patients.

In spite all of my professional training and experience, with each of the soldiers I treated I found myself feeling heartsick. Although I was only in my early thirties, I felt that any one of them could have been my son. It was difficult to be devoid of any emotions in caring for these poor boys.

It was an honor for me to serve with these Israeli colleagues and with Dr. Kazlov, who was British—even with Uram, who told me what he thought of us Americans, in general, as medical practitioners. He was a brilliant technician, in spite of his attitude. I remained at this station, under Dr. Kazlov's caring and well-qualified command, for forty-eight hours. Though a semi-armistice was in effect, Syrian tanks were within view of our forces on the other side of the border. That, coupled with the bitter weather, caused the Scandinavian United Nations troops that were stationed there to quit their positions, leaving us to cope with the enemy on our own. Several of us were suffering from frostbite of the face and extremities in spite of our heavy garb. Never having had a tolerance for severe cold, I begged leave of Dr. Kazlov and his colleagues and headed for a post farther south, at the Beer Sheva hospital in the Sinai.

The strain on the medical corps there was tremendous. Some of us had worked up to forty-eight-hour shifts, taking catnaps at intervals. I got to working a seventy-hour work week, plus on occasion relieving other overburdened nurses. Tempers flared short as casualties continued to pour in, with the casualties and the regular patients lying three litters across through the entire length of some corridors, with no privacy whatever. Intravenous infusions, dressings, and bedpans had to be given under these circumstances, with almost no room for doctors and nurses to move around. We were grossly understaffed and overburdened, and the casualties kept coming in to us. One must keep in mind that there were about three million of us Israelis pitted against over eighty million enemies from the Arab states, and often we were expected (medical as well as military personnel) to take on three times the responsibilities of one nurse, medic, or soldier. We were all physically and emotionally drained to the limit. We did not smell too good after a while either, as there was no time for showers or changes of clothes. Every second meant the possible saving or loss of a human life.

Some of the worst casualties were the tankists, who had been severely scorched by the Egyptian suicide squads. For a tankist, the chief parts of the body exposed are the hands and head. Some of the boys had received seventh-degree burns. (At that time, burn categories extended from first to seventh degrees, seventh being intensely charred burns, often straight to the bone, resembling an extremely overdone charcoal-broiled steak. If the readers find this a somewhat extreme analogy, let them imagine the horrendous effect it had on us as rescuers, and especially on the poor sufferers of these burns.) They usually had been hit by missiles from shoulder-held rocket launchers, wielded by drugged Arab soldiers at extremely close range. What was left of the tankists' faces, necks, and hands looked like a hot water bottle that had been badly burned, like a spectre out of a horror movie, only this horror was real. The plastic surgeons worked feverishly on those whose lives could be saved, some of whom would need at least sixteen plastic grafts and repairs. In many cases though, the tankists' fingertips had been completely burned off, so that they could never use their hands again. They had to be cleaned after the toilet, washed, fed, and dressed. Try to envision what it was like for men between the ages of eighteen and twenty-five, many of whom were married and had two or three children, to be turned into totally dependent beings for the rest of their lives.

Among all of the triage cases, one particularly stands out in my memory. It was that of an eighteen-year-old Yemenite Jewish soldier, Shimon, who had been hit by a combination of bullets and shrapnel in the right chest. His right lung was essentially gone, and Malka, the Argentinian respiratory therapist and I were trying desperately to get Shimon to take deep breaths. This was done to keep his remaining left lung, which had also been injured, functioning, while he screamed in agony. The problem was that we could give him only a minimal dose of morphine for the pain, because morphine depresses respirations. Malka managed to keep a stiff upper lip throughout the procedures, but I felt a huge golf ball well up in my throat as I continued to work on Shimon with her. In the meantime, Shimon's beautiful (beautiful of face as well as spirit) forty-year-old mother stood, choked up, yet stoic, in the open doorway of the recovery room. As I left Shimon's bedside with another nurse in charge, I had to pass by her. This lady took my hands in hers and pleadingly asked me in Hebrew, "Do you think my son will get better? Do you think, nurse, that he will live?" I could only answer, "I hope so. May G-d be with you," after which I went into our coffee break room and wept. After all, what do you say to a mother whose son is in critical condition, in extreme pain, and whose chances of surviving are very slim? When you know that he is losing blood as fast as it is being transfused into him, and she is watching life slowly draining from her child, what do you say to a mother?

Under normal circumstances, when a patient died, it would be the physician's job to inform the family of the patient's death. Sometimes in those awful wartime days, nurses, rabbis, and others were given the duty of having to inform families that they had just lost a son or a daughter. To my regret, though I hoped he lived, I do not know exactly what became of Shimon, as he was later transferred to another, acute care unit, and we were too busy with new casualties to always be able to check on the old ones. Life was like that in those days.

As if that scene were not bad enough, there was a spinal cord injury ward, one of the most depressing places one could ever be. Here were a large number of young men, most of whom had been hit by shrapnel at the base of the skull or neck. Of all body tissues, there is no repair for damaged brain or spinal cord tissue. The one saving grace, if it can be called that, was that almost all of these boys were unconscious. Their grim-faced parents, spouses, brothers, and sisters sat in a lounge room off the ward. I have pretty strong control in medical situations, but this heart-rending scene caused me to burst into tears as soon as I left the unit. There was no hope for these young men of regaining consciousness or recovering their mobility—only the question of how long they would linger in this vegetative state.

Moreover, at the Soroka Hospital in Beer Sheva, often we would have a blackout in the event of an enemy raid. Also, power outages occurred. Only the operating suites and the emergency room had emergency power generators. All the rest of the hospital had to work by flashlights and candles. I do not know how many medical colleagues can envision us having to intubate patients with one sterile, gloved hand while we held a dripping wax candle in the other hand. Many nurses and medics performed procedures that they normally would not have performed, because most of the doctors were behind the front lines or in the operating rooms. We had three to six times more casualties and regular patients than we were equipped to accommodate. A touch of humor must not be left out of this scene of chaos. Suddenly one of the patients stopped breathing. The chief of respiratory, Dr. Pesarovitch, calmly said in Yiddish, *"Gib im a bessele luft,"* which means "Give him a little bit of air." Of course we gave the patient oxygen right away, and he revived. It is amazing, through all the pathos, how the Jewish sense of humor holds steadfast.

One aspect of the war that must be mentioned, however, is the treatment of Israeli prisoners of war by Arab captors, the worst having been the Syrians and Iraqis. Application of electric shocks, beatings, and burning cigarettes on their bodies were practiced on Israelis taken captive. The terms of care of enemy prisoners of war in the Geneva Accord were seldom observed, unlike Israel's care of enemy wounded. They received medical care as fine as any of our own soldiers. Most of the enemy wounded did not even say thank-you in Arabic.

As if the devastation of war were not enough, severe rainstorms accompanied by mudslides added to the suffering of many. I distinctly remember one poor Bedouin woman, whose husband was away, being brought to the emergency unit with her four children, all covered with mud. A mudslide had collapsed their tent on top of them, and they had walked several miles till a kind passerby noticed them, picked them up in his car, and brought them in. They had not eaten for hours, so they were placed near a space heater to dry off and given some basic staples to eat and drink, till the storm died down. I took exception to a man's standing near them holding his nose, because of the odor of the wood fire smoke, which is common to Bedouins. People need to be more culturally tolerant.

The severe weather, combined with the shortage of manpower, wreaked havoc in more ways than one. Public transportation, especially in busy districts and at rush hour, turned the central bus station of Tel Aviv, which is usually chaotic anyway, into a quagmire of overcrowded buses in a gigantic traffic jam, which at one point did not move for about half an hour. Some men had just been grabbed off the street to drive buses, and the driver on whose bus I was had no idea about what route to take. Fortunately, some of the passengers knew the route well and kept directing and redirecting the poor man, who, in a state of great nervousness (who wouldn't be), kept making wrong turns. In addition, the visibility was poor, and the rain continued to pour in torrents. One irate passenger shouted in Hebrew, "That man doesn't know where the hell he is in the world." Also, as many of the regular transit buses had to be put into service for emergency military use, we were short of buses. Thus, on our bus alone, at least an extra hundred passengers were jammed into spaces, including doorways.

In addition, a three-year-old girl accidentally got separated from her father, and one kind Iraqi Jew said that he and his wife would take the child home and care for her, if her family didn't show up. Luckily, the bewildered father made his way to the child just before the end of the bus trip. In the meantime, the little girl had a nice nap in the Iraqi woman's arms. We got smashed in the ribs often during the jolting, packed, confusing bus trip. I was so sore afterwards, as we pulled into Rehovot.

During a similar trip at that time, I recall a very brave and accomplished young woman (who could not have been over twenty) masterfully driving a giant tractor down the road from the kibbutz. She was wearing denim overalls, a long-sleeved sport shirt, and a kerchief on her head. She had an air of dignity about her as she made a difficult turn in the road, very skillfully. The man standing next to me on the bus marveled at her, even though he, too, was a *sabra*, or native-born Israeli, and had known women to do difficult work on the kibbutzim.

As for deeds of valor, my greatest admiration went to my colleague nurse, Batya, from Tunisia. She was an ace at handling emergencies under the worst of circumstances. For the benefit of any Western colleagues who doubt the professional abilities of Oriental Jews in Israel, they could learn much from Batya. Without batting an eyelash, she cared for her own patients, as well as helping me, with nerves of steel, to place airways, control hemorrhaging, and do up the isolation patients. (We had one patient with encephalitis, which is potentially lethal and extremely infectious.) We had to traverse a long, open corridor to get to our unit, and Batya dragged me along, through the pouring rain and hailstones that tore at our faces and uniforms. In the process, we both came down violently ill, I with sinusitis and she with pneumonia. Batya had a fever of 104°F and I had one of 103°F. At one stage of the game Batya was so sick that she was coughing up blood, but would not give in to herself, and continued to care for patients. She set an example for me, and I followed suit, till we both succumbed and had to be relieved. We were treated, put on heavy doses of antibiotics, and sent home. Then the water main was damaged and for twenty-four hours there was no drinking water as we lay in our beds, parched, with fevers tearing at us. We were lucky, though. We made it through.

Others were less fortunate. Most Israeli housing then, especially the old, stone buildings of the 1940's, did not have central heating, and many of the homes in the villages had only makeshift windows or shutters. The inhabitants used a foul-smelling, smoky kerosene space heater on wheels, which they moved from one room to the next to warm the house. Under these conditions, many of the children came down with repeated bouts of strep throat, and though the local doctors put them on penicillin or erythromycin, the children often relapsed, and some developed rheumatic heart disease. Some would later need open-heart surgery to correct valvular defects. The unusually cold, severe winter contributed appreciably to the worsening of these conditions, and the suffering was intense.

There was one week in early February 1974 when it rained non-stop. By day and by night the rain came in torrents, with intermittent hailstorms that tore at the flesh of men and beasts. A peddler who made his only livelihood by selling housewares door-to-door got caught in the storm with his horse and cart, and kind neighbors had to help him out of the mud. He did no more peddling that week. The rains continued unabated, pelting, blinding, driving the spirit out of a person. In addition, there was the suffering of cattle and chickens, though the farmers made every effort to protect them. Many crops were badly damaged too, including some banana plantations, and low-lying farms with poor drainage took heavy losses.

For some strange reason catastrophes seem to come in clusters, when we are least able to cope with them. Next came a poultry disease for which there were no inoculations. Many chickens had to be killed to prevent spread of the disease. Consequently, our supply of fresh poultry and eggs was sharply curtailed. Most of it was saved for the sick and wounded. It took almost a year to bring the disease under control. We take so much for granted in America, such as having eggs for breakfast every day, and feeling free to make a sponge cake with eight eggs in it. I have never taken such things for granted since.

A word of credit for the unsung heroines of the war is now due. Throughout the thick of battle, the volunteer women of W.I.Z.O. (Women's International Zionist Organization), many of them quite old, baked cakes and all sorts of pastries by day and by night, to be given to other W.I.Z.O. women who lined the main roads of battle. With their baskets of pastries and coffee urns and sandwiches, they fed the exhausted, battle-weary soldiers. I am very proud to say that my cousin, Lola Weil (of blessed memory), was among these women.

There is one more important point to be brought out here, that of the element of color and national background in Israel, which did not matter as we fought and suffered side by side during the Yom Kippur War. Thus I found it refreshing in peacetime also, where religion, not color, make a difference, primarily regarding marriage. In the Middle East it is practically unthinkable for a man and a woman of different faiths to intermarry, though no one gets upset when people of the same faith but different national origins marry. After all, color is only skin deep, and what matters it if the bride comes from England and the groom from the Jews of Ethiopia or Persia? What does matter is that they both love Israel, as well as each other. As Jews, though we have different dress and culinary customs, and some differences in Passover observances, it is a diversity that enriches rather than divides us.

TEN

BEDOUINS AND THE DESERT

THERE WAS ONE LAST EXPERIENCE I HAD DURING THE WAR THAT EDUCATED ME GREATLY. That was while I did nursing in the south of Israel, in Beer Sheva. Beer Sheva then had barely the rudimentary form of a city, with the beginning of construction of a shopping mall at the central bus station. I am told it has since blossomed into quite a thriving, modern community.

This is definitely where the world of three thousand years ago and the twenty-first century meet. Within a twenty-minute walk of the central bus station was the desert shuk, made up of old Sephardi shops (butchers, grocers, jewelers, fabric shops, and the Yemenite holy articles store) and every Thursday, the Bedouin open market. On that day Bedouins would come in from their tents in the desert to sell hand-crafted jewelry, hand-made embroidered navy blue and black velvet dresses, eggs of wild birds, camel skin bags, pottery, and a variety of other exotic items. I bought and ate a few Bedouin eggs (which my future husband later told me were non-kosher and therefore forbidden to Jews) and found them delicious!

As for garments, I cannot understand how the Bedouin woman can wear heavy black velvet dresses during the summer in temperatures of over a hundred degrees, but the hand embroidery on the dresses is exquisite. I also like the Bedouin circular hanging earrings, in gold or silver, and to this day I have two such pairs. Unfortunately, the costliness of the women's beautiful headdresses, necklaces, and bracelets made these items out of the question for me.

I was privileged, through a Bedouin friend of one of my roommates at Ulpan Etzion, to acquire some knowledge of Bedouin life and society. The young man, later to become Dr. Yunis, the first Bedouin to graduate from a university of Western medicine, and an excellent internist, was of the Bedouin village of Kfar Abu-Raavia. When last I spoke with Dr. Yunis, he was determined to upgrade the standards of health teaching and general health for all of his people. That was very briefly in 1974. Our relations were strained, as he knew that I had returned to help my people in a war against his people, and that made me feel very bad. I shall always have great respect for Dr. Yunis, both as a gentleman and as a physician. I recall the stories told me by mutual friends, of the great party his late father held in his honor for graduating from medical school. The menu included *munsaf,* a meal consisting of an entire roast goat or sheep stuffed with a chicken and laid upon a bed of rice, which in turn is placed on a huge pita bread. Every Bedouin relative and dignitary around was invited to the event. I should have liked to have been present, too.

Regarding the Bedouin tribal setup, each tribe owns its individual *dirah* of desert, an area that could be many miles across, usually containing several wells. These wells are quite primitive, without any covering, and the water is often polluted. The Bedouin tents are usually of goat hair, with the women's and children's quarters separated by a curtain from the men's quarters. The people rely on their camels, goats, and sheep for most of their basic needs, including milk and cheese, as well as using camel dung as fuel. Now and then the Bedouin and other Arab women, accompanied by their children, would come by the Jewish butchers in town. I felt so sorry for them when I saw them buying turkey heads to cook with *ful* (a kind of bean), garlic, onions, and spices, and serve with rice. The rest of their staples are dates and a gruel made of corn, millet, or sorghum. When locusts are in abundance, they are put into a stew or dried and then eaten. Coffee is laboriously hand-ground and is very strong and sweet, I am told, though I have never drunk it. The feasts are first presented on the men's side of the tent, and then the women are allowed to finish whatever is left by the men, everyone using his or her right hand to eat.

It is also a custom of the Bedouins to place a glob of mud on the raw umbilicus of a newborn child, thereby presumably ensuring the survival of the fittest. However, after several medical colleagues and I watched Bedouin babies go into opisthotonos (convulsions with the whole back arched), notwithstanding medication we had given them for tetanus, and then die, we could not accept that custom. It is only within limits that one can intrude into another people's deeply ingrained beliefs, though.

I also felt sorry for the married Bedouin women, wearing cumbersome gold rings pierced through the right sides of their noses. This is according to Old Testament custom (of Rebecca, who was given a gold nose jewel of gold by Eliezer, the servant of Isaac, whom she then married). This is part of the marriage custom (among other Arab peoples also), for the groom and his family to present the bride with a variety of gold bracelets, necklaces, and nose jewels, as a kind of insurance, should the husband ever decide to desert his wife and their children.

As I cared for the Bedouin women and children as patients, I found them very receptive to personal caring and sincerity. From the Bedouins, as well as from my husband, I learned about the desert—to appreciate and respect it, its creatures, and its life. To begin with, the word *sahara* means "emptiness" in Arabic, and this aptly describes most deserts. Along with other tourists and native Israelis going on a guided tour in the Negev (which means without water) Desert, I came to appreciate some of the desert's characteristics. Unlike the Sahara, here and there were cacti, shrubs, and other plants. We were told that in times of great drought certain cacti are cut open and their bitter liquid is sucked out in place of water. Some cacti are poisonous, though, and should be touched only by a skilled desert traveler. Some Westerners have unfortunately decided to try desert travel on their own and have never returned. Even the Bedouins go in pairs in the desert, though they are probably among the world's best trackers. To a Bedouin, every bent blade of grass, every broken twig, every footprint means something valuable in tracking.

The desert holds many dangers for the inexperienced traveler, however. The desert's shifting sands often make any trail impossible to follow. There is also quicksand, for which reason the Bedouins will sometimes have a mule precede them, so that if the animal is suddenly sucked up by this hidden death, they can go around the area. Then too, there are desert sand storms, sometimes severe. Another woman and I were once caught up in one such storm in the market in Beer Sheva, and for a few brief, frightening moments, we were lifted with all of our crates of eggs up off the ground into the air. Then we were dropped back down to earth and landed on our feet, luckily. It is for such reasons that Arab people wear the head cloth called the burnoose, to wrap about one's face during a sandstorm, as well as for esthetics. Likewise, nature has endowed camels with a second set of eyelids, which are impervious to sand but still allow them to see. Another danger in the desert, towards the rainy season, is sudden severe downpours, which can turn a barren area into a quagmire of mud. If one is in a depression below a high sand dune, one can be engulfed by this kind of avalanche. These downpours are rare, but when they occur, they are intense. It is also at these times that the plants and animals of the desert absorb all the precious water that they can, many of them being equipped to store liquid for some time. It is after such rains that the desert plants begin to bloom, and all life there takes advantage of the opportunity to reproduce, so that the offspring can thrive.

As for other dangers of the desert, mirages can occur in the daytime, as optical illusions are caused by hot air over the sands. If one is lost or alone, one can imagine one's name being called or other familiar sounds. However, the sounds of the night can be much more disconcerting. These sounds are produced by the sands cooling off at night, and by piles of sand sliding down steep dunes, causing a booming sound. Some of the dunes can be as high as a tall hill or small mountain. These sounds can also resemble wailing voices, which, combined with the yelping of hyenas, barks of jackals, and slithering sounds of reptiles, can be enough to unnerve the most stalwart people.

Seasoned desert dwellers are not particularly disturbed by these choruses, but the novice traveler can be quite shaken by them. As for attacks by venomous pit vipers and yellow scorpions, these animals are much more afraid of humans than we are of them, but have been known to attack in the dark. The spiders, millipedes, and lizards are not dangerous at all. Moreover, these creatures are very important parts of the ecological chain that maintains a plant to insect to reptile to carnivore and man cycle for the maintenance of life in the desert. Israelis and Arabs rarely wantonly kill snakes or other creatures, as they understand their benefit to the environment in general.

The desert teems with life, from the hundreds of varieties of insects and arthropods that make their homes in cacti and burrows, to the hawks, wrens, and other birds that eat insects and rodents, to the jackals and other predators that make up the desert community. Even beetles, such as dung beetles, have their own function in this place. Many animals have special adaptations to conserve water, such as extra fat pads beneath the skin, or very thick skin that does not allow the moisture to evaporate readily.

As for geographical beauty, during our tour in the Negev, we got to see some beautifully colored mountains, with sometimes bizarre shapes formed by hundreds of years of wind and sand erosion. In the Negev there were frequently interspersed patches of grass, desert flowers, and shrubs growing wild. When sunset fell in the desert, it was preceded by only a brief twilight, but with a commanding air, as if to say, "This land must be let alone, that no man may touch it."

ELEVEN

JERUSALEM AND MARRIAGE

AFTER MY EXPERIENCES WITH BEDOUINS, AS I WAS SERVING IN BEER SHEVA DURING THE YOM KIPPUR WAR, FINALLY AN ARMISTICE WAS SIGNED BETWEEN ISRAEL AND ITS WARRING NEIGHBORS. Then I had a chance for a respite from my nursing duties, and decided I wanted to be where there was culture, in Jerusalem. Though I have not been to every capital in the world, I cannot imagine any other being more beautiful than Jerusalem. In the refrain of the song "Jerusalem of Gold" is mentioned not only Jerusalem of gold, but also of copper and light. This refers to East Jerusalem, when seen from adjacent hills at sunset, giving impressions of copper and of light. The gold-painted rooftop of the mosque known as the Dome of the Rock glistens as if it were of pure gold in the sun's fading rays. The ivy-covered walls of the synagogues, mosques, and churches, add a touch of verdure.

This shimmering beauty, in combination with the plaintive sound of the *muezzins* of the mosques calling the faithful to prayer in their minor key, adds to the unique ambiance of Jerusalem. The Jewish men, coming to Maariv prayers in the evening, wearing their *tallitim* (prayer shawls) as they enter the synagogues, complete the religious essence of Jerusalem at sunset. As I think back to the wonders of Jerusalem, I think of Mount Zion, whose ancient Crusaders' stone walls enclose King David's tomb and, adjacent to it, the dimly lit memorial reminder of the Nazi death camps. Not far away is the Lion's Gate (so-called from a lion's statue on either side). From atop Mount Zion we look down on the poetic beauty of the Quidron Valley, with ancient stone ruins alongside old Arab cemeteries.

From the outskirts of the Katamon section of Jerusalem, where my girlfriend Dina and I lived, we could see a few sparse stone houses on the hills, inhabited mostly by Moroccan Jews, and beyond that the area called the German colony, founded by Jews from that country. The Baqa section follows, heading toward the West Bank. To the left are several hills carefully terraced by Arab farmers, with vineyards and fig trees, which take a long time to grow. I hope that this area has remained intact since I left Israel. Beyond is the breathtaking view of the Judean Desert and the mountains that border Jordan, in all their majestic brown, gray, and purple.

I also think back to my late mother-in-law's house and the view from the rear porch of her second-floor apartment, looking at the grass- and stone-covered hills—Jordanian hills before 1967, now belonging to Israel. Beyond that are hills stretching out almost to Tel Aviv. I can still visualize the purple and gold sunset shining on those hills, with a few Arab villages, and sheep and goats grazing.

Within that area is Yaar Yerushalayim (the Jerusalem Forest), where Simon and I used to enjoy many walks together when we were engaged. In the summer the forest's trees and plants blend with the wild flowers to create a perfume of nature's own. The road, several kilometers long, passes through patches of wild mushrooms and abundant *charoov* (carob) trees, which, according to my husband, Simon, are an excellent source of cattle fodder, as well as a substitute for chocolate in cooking. The view from halfway up the forest road not only includes our former home and cottages, but also extends far into the hills that separate Jerusalem from Tel Aviv. There are several memorials on this path also, including the large stone one erected by Hannah Druyan in memory of her late husband and son. Hannah Druyan is a Jerusalem philanthropist whose husband died suddenly on hearing of the accidental death of their son in the Israeli army. She is one of the finest ladies I have ever known.

In the Jerusalem Forest, as elsewhere in Israel, there are poisonous as well as non-poisonous snakes and lizards, many of which are very graceful.

There are scorpions, too, including the yellow, lethal variety, which come out mostly at night. The black variety deliver a very painful sting that can make a person sick for a few days, but the bite is non-lethal. Even in the more densely populated cities, the gardens teem with reptiles, some of them venomous.

The people, especially some of the voluble Sephardi shopkeepers of the Mahane Yehuda shuk, will always stand out in my memory. Mr. Kaduri, the Iraqi banana vendor, with his stand at the corner of Mahane Yehuda and Agrippas Street, had a kind greeting for everyone. He would never overcharge a customer even one *grush,* which is about the equivalent of one penny in American money. All the vendors with whom my husband and I dealt, for that matter, were very honest people. The shuk was at the top of the hill that runs parallel to Yaffo Street, one of the main streets of Jerusalem. Basically, most of Jerusalem, including the business districts, is composed of a series of successively higher, rolling hills. The view from many of these hills is rich, such as the view from the Mount of Olives, which looks down on an Arab village of small stone houses and an old cemetery adjacent to it.

It is also beautiful to look down on Arab villages with their terraced vineyards and Arabs leading their flocks of sheep and goats to graze. The men are attired in their ankle-length robes with a cord around the waist and a loose robe in front, with the traditional burnoose head cloth. The most cherished hill to the Jews, though, is the one in East Jerusalem that is behind the Western Wailing Wall of the holy Temple of Solomon. Because no one knows exactly where the Temple and the Holiest of Holies (the Ark of the Covenant) stood, it is considered sacrilegious for observant Jews to cross over behind the Wall to visit the Mosque of Omar.

Getting back to the Sephardi shopkeepers of the Mahane Yehuda shuk, diagonally across the street from Mr. Kaduri's banana stand was the tiny housewares shop belonging to the Aharons. Both Mr. and Mrs. Aharon were short of stature with dusky features and a delightful sense of humor. How the Aharons ever managed to find a saucepan or candelabrum in their cluttered shop, with layers of kitchenware and religious items on top of more layers, is beyond me. As a husband and wife team eking out a living, they were both incredibly funny and helpful. Mr. Aharon always had the best suggestions on how to repair broken panels or door hinges for his clients. However, his wife often chimed in (and truthfully so), "He always gives advice to everyone else on how to fix things, but do you think he ever lifts a finger to repair our house? Never! The Messiah will come before my husband does one thing around the house." And yet with all the trivial bickering, it was obvious what a loving couple these people were.

I also enjoyed philosophizing with the Aharons. They, especially Mr. Aharon, had some pithy comments to make as to why people should be less self-centered and more giving in the name of the Torah. The Aharons were also deeply pious, keeping the Sabbath and doing a good deed whenever they could. At the risk of making less money, Mrs. Aharon, with her broad smile, once told me not to buy a particular soup ladle but rather to buy a cheaper one that was of better quality. The world needs so many more people like the Aharons.

From memories of the streets off Mahane Yehuda near the Aharons' shop, I can still recall the aromas of falafel and *shawarma* (roast lamb, cooking slowly in thick slices on a huge, upright skewer), all coming from the local restaurants, and the fragrant smell of Turkish coffee.

As for culture, Jerusalem's Museum of Semitic History claims some of Judaism's and the Orient's finest relics. These include the floor-length, white linen Yemenite bridal dress, exquisitely hand-embroidered with pearls, gems, and gold and silver thread, with the outer portion also embroidered in gold and silver. Accompanying it is the matching twenty-kilogram bridal headdress, overlaid with an opulent silver filigree crown, with many strands of richly designed silver extending from one side of the bride's head to the other, and hanging under her chin.

Also enshrined here are Turkish, Indian, Italian, and German Torah scrolls, encased in gold, silver, and brass respectively, with the motifs of their cultures, some dating back as far a thousand years or more. These are accompanied by candelabra, kiddush cups in hand-carved silver, incense burners used to bring the Sabbath to a close, and Passover seder plates, all hand-decorated in silver and gold, and many other religious relics from Jewish communities all over the world.

Enshrined in separate showcases are the costumes worn by Jews from many different cultures. There is the attire of the Georgian Jews, the men's full trousers gathered at the waist and ankles and baggy shirts tucked into the trousers, all fastened by cummerbunds, plus round caps with lovely embroidery. The women are garbed in full, gathered skirts with ribbon trimming on the bottom, covered by embroidered aprons, with white puffy-sleeved blouses tucked into them. The Jewesses of Hadramaut in Southern Arabia wear baggy women's trousers heavily embroidered on the bottom, covered by colorful long skirts, with blouses and tunics, also rich with hand embroidery, and long headdresses. The Jewesses of Hadramaut are also known for their very fine carpet work. Next come the long, flowing robes and headdresses of the Bedouin men and women (the women's being exquisitely embroidered). Exhibits of Semitic handicrafts include intricate basket work, swords with finely carved handles, fine pottery, embroidered linens, and exquisitely chiseled jewelry in gold, silver, and ivory, among other crafts. Here, in short, are exhibited the most meaningful aspects of both Jewish and Arabic culture.

All of these places—the Jerusalem Museum of Semitic History, the Jerusalem Forest, and Jerusalem's many historical and religious shrines and sites—are on a par with Boston's Museum of Fine Arts and its Arnold Arboretum.

In Jerusalem I met Tsila and Yehiel, a Soviet Jewish couple, as we were traveling on the same train. They had both been through a Nazi concentration camp, as well as a Soviet prison camp, so they had more than their share of misery in their backgrounds. They were both short and in their early seventies. Tsila had a twinkle in her eyes, wore glasses, and had short, gray, wavy hair. Yehiel was solidly built, with wavy gray hair complementing his very perceptive dark eyes. They had come to Israel a short time before, to live with with their divorced daughter and her twin little girls in Nahariya. Tsila always had a good sense of humor; Yehiel was the critical one. In particular, he often criticized Tsila, who unfortunately was getting progressively more deaf. Tsila was the first one to observe, as they visited with Simon and me, that my future mother-in-law would ruin our marriage. Essentially, Tsila and Yehiel mutually adopted me, and we kept a strong bond together for quite some time. Among other things, we shopped in the Arab shuk in East Jerusalem, took long walks, and talked over plans for our future in Israel.

Then, having gotten a job at Hadassah Hospital and having Passover off, I decided to visit my old friends, the Weisses, in Rehovot. Rehovot is one of the most attractive cities in Israel, with clothing, jewelry, shoe, and all-purpose stores lining its modern streets, together with the usual falafel and soft drink cafes. As I dashed to catch the last bus out of Jerusalem, another young woman, Sarah Cohen, was rushing with me, and we teamed up for the trip. She told me she was headed for her sister Rachel's home in the village of Bnai Ayeesh. She said she was sure her sister and family would welcome me, and so I should feel free to come. In Israel people are friendly that way, often without formal invitations.

As I had already been invited by the Weisses, I went to them first. Rivka and Yaakov Weiss and I met in the United States in a Boston hospital, where Yaakov was being treated for esophageal strictures, which he had endured as a prisoner of the Nazis, from the human experiments to which many of the inmates were subjected. Other friends and I who worked at the hospital and belonged to the Jewish Defense League, visited Yaakov often to help feed him and translate for him. Unfortunately, poor Yaakov died upon returning to Israel. Rivka and I remained friends, though. Rivka, a short woman whose head was always covered by an Orthodox cloth, had invited me to visit with them when I returned to Israel. She then had two grown children, Abraham, who was married, and Dina who was yet single. From downtown Rehovot I traveled by bus to the plateau-like *shicun* where the Weisses lived. Their spacious three-room cottage, one of the original ones erected when Israel became a state, was bright and airy. Each cottage had a large garden in front of it, giving the whole area an atmosphere of pastoral quietude.

I had been graciously hosted by the Weiss family when I arrived in Israel at the outset of the war, and I remember their sharing. Rivka's son, Abraham, with his wife Henia and their infant son, had come to spend Passover with her, and we all had a lovely holiday, each pitching in with the chores. Rivka's neighbors all greeted me cordially, as well. They came from Czechoslovakia, Poland, Morocco, and Yemen.

After spending the first days of Passover with the Weisses, I thanked them and headed for Kfar (village) Bnai Ayeesh. The Sephardi families there are very Orthodox, and so all have very large families. The smallest family had nine children, the largest, seventeen. It was obvious that people there were very poor; some wore tattered clothes, and some of the cottages had no windowpanes. In spite of this, Rachel Cohen and her family greeted me with warmth and generosity. Though Rachel was a bit overweight, she was exquisitely beautiful, even without any make-up. Her coloring was medium brown, with dark eyes and jet-black hair that was neatly tucked under her kerchief and tied at the back of her head. Her arched eyebrows, straight nose, and fine lips completed her beauty. Six of us slept abreast in a bed built for two, but it was a small inconvenience in comparison with the love and hospitality I received. Rachel immediately took me into her kitchen to help her cook and prepare vegetables, while she chatted with her sister, Sarah, and me about how to find me a good Jewish husband. We must all keep in mind that Jewish mothers are innate matchmakers.

All of Rachel's and the other villagers' children were extremely polite, which is in contrast to the average sabra or, for that matter, local Bostonian youngsters. When I was ready to return to Jerusalem, Rachel loaded me up with a variety of fruits, meats, and cakes, much of which had been grown and prepared in the village. She had to make sure that I would not be hungry on the way. I did not want to take it from her, because of their circumstances, but Rachel said she would feel very offended if I did not. Rachel treated me as a sister while I was there. There is truly no more loving hospitality in the world than Sephardic Jewish hospitality.

As Sarah and I were returning to Jerusalem, she said she thought she could match me up with a roommate, and gave me her number. That was how Dina Sida and her family and I met. I moved into her apartment and we got along fine, to the point that her family adopted me. They are Iraqi Jews and also very warm, outgoing people. Like Rachel Cohen, the Sidas set about looking for a husband for me. They insisted that whatever family event they attended, I had to go with them and Dina. Thus it was one evening when Dina suddenly told me there was to be a wedding in the family, and I had to come. At that moment I was in the shower and my hair was wet. She said it did not matter, and I should just put on my pretty, red Sephardi tunic and trousers suit. In this unattractive state, with my hair soaking wet, I got into a car driven by Galia and Yitzhak (Dina's brother and sister-in-law) with Dina, and off we went to Aperion Hall.

After the ceremony, as I danced with Dina's brothers, Galia suddenly told me she thought she had a prospective husband for me. With all of the hubbub of the crowd, I tried to remember which man Galia had pointed out to me. When I had been introduced to Simon, I said *"Shalom,"* and kept on going. Then Galia and her sister-in-law, Hela, got together and asked me if

I would go along with a formal introduction, to which I said yes. My future husband, Simon, and I then met and spoke at length in a nook of the catering hall, and were mutually drawn to each other like two peas in a pod. At that time Simon was smashingly handsome (which was not the reason I married him), about five feet eight inches tall, with wavy, jet black hair, intense dark brown eyes, and finely chiseled cheekbones. He was wearing black trousers and a white, short-sleeved shirt with a black design on it.

For my part, I have never been exceptionally attractive. When I am fully made up and have my hair done up in an elevated coiffure, I am fairly attractive, with ash blonde hair, green eyes, and fair skin. I stand at five feet, seven inches tall. At the time I met Simon, I had a very good figure (I have put on another thirty pounds since then). The conversation in Aperion Hall went very well, with our mutually conservative interests, our liking for (East) Indian foods and culture, and our interest in medicine. A date was set for the following week. Simon and his friend Joab accidentally arrived late, having lost the directions, and I remember how Simon bolted up the stairs to make up for it. Our first date at an outdoor play, an art shop, and a restaurant was heavenly, after which Simon had to get me to my night-shift job at Hadassah Hospital. He asked my permission to kiss me goodnight, and I granted it. I had never before done that with a man on a first date.

Somehow I knew then and there that Simon was going to be my husband, so the goodnight kiss was acceptable. Unbelievably enough, after that first date, Simon invited me to spend the following Sabbath with him and his mother, which invitation I accepted, and we started to make marriage plans two months later. At that point his mother seemed pleased with me. Simon was then a master accountant and had had a steady job with the Jewish National Fund for almost twenty years. My one mistake in our marriage was looking at the situation through "rose-colored glasses." I should have discussed openly with Simon the possibility of moving elsewhere if things did not work out with his mother living with us. Of course, hindsight is always easier than foresight. It then seemed unfathomable that Simon's diminutive mother, seemingly very quiet and reserved, could end up destroying our marriage.

What many Americans do not realize is that many Israelis are forced into extended kinship home situations because of economics. Thus many young couples wind up living with in-laws, not always by choice. In the

United States one usually rents an apartment or buys a house; in Israel one usually buys an apartment. Only the very wealthy buy a house in the Middle East, as it is extremely expensive.

Simon and I had a beautiful wedding ceremony at the Yochanan Ben Zakkai synagogue in East Jerusalem. This ancient synagogue is composed of four Sephardi synagogues, the oldest being named for the prophet Eliyahu HaNavi. Legend has it that many years ago there were only nine men to pray on the Day of Atonement, failing to make a *minyan* (quorum) of ten men. Suddenly an old man joined the group in the morning and disappeared after nightfall, leading all to believe that the stranger had been Elijah the Prophet. After that the next addition to the synagogues was called Kahal Kadosh Gadol (Great Congregation), where Rabbi Yochanan Ben Zakkai taught.[1]

Simon and I on our wedding day, August 15, 1974, outside the Yochanan Ben Zakkai synagogue in the Old City of Jerusalem, with the old city walls and the minarets of a Muslim mosque in the background.

The Rabbi lived at the time of the brutal regime of the Roman emperor Vespasian, renowned for his crucifixion of thousands of Jewish men, women, and children. Seeing the worst about to come, Rabbi Yochanan had himself smuggled out of Jerusalem in a coffin, and then managed to get to speak with Vespasian's son, Titus. The rabbi was so successful that Titus allowed him to found a school for the study of Torah at Jabneh, near Jaffa, with full spiritual authority over the Jews throughout Palestine. Shortly thereafter, Jerusalem fell and the Temple was destroyed. After that Rabbi Yochanan and his associates devoted themselves to the study of Hebrew law and scriptures. This came to be called the *Mishnah,* also known as *Halakha,* or "way of life." After that many additions were made to the Mishnah by the Jews of the Persian Empire. Also included was the *Haggadah,* a compilation of Hebrew history, medicine, ethics, sciences, and biography.[2]

This great collection of Hebrew law, history, and way of life has come to comprise the Talmud, which has also been put down in writing, so that Jews since then have had a religious and ethical basis for their lives and communities throughout the world. Thanks to the great self-sacrifice and efforts of Rabbi Yochanan Ben Zakkai and others like him, the Hebrew people have the Talmud to fall back on in times of need. Thus the Hebrew people are known as "The People of the Book."[3]

The Istanbuli Congregation was next added to the synagogue, consisting of Jews whose ancestors had fled the Spanish Inquisition. They brought their religion and culture with them to the North African lands, such as Morocco and Tunisia. Though the Muslim rulers who occupied the Middle East, including Palestine during the seventeenth century, were not always tolerant of other religions, they were far more tolerant than the Christian rulers. With the advent of the Ottoman rule returning to Palestine in 1840, the Chief Rabbi of Israel, known as Rishon LeZion (First of Zion), received full respect for his status. He was revered by the Sultan as Hacham Bashi. From then on the inauguration of the Chief Rabbi took place in the Yochanan Ben Zakkai synagogue, highly regarded by both Sephardi and Ashkenazim. (Pilgrims to Jerusalem were always called up to read the Hebrew law here also.)

Last to be added to the synagogues was the Emtzai (Middle) or Zion Congregation, the smallest in the group, which is said to be connected to the Hebrew royal tombs. The construction of all the above synagogues began about four hundred years ago. The most recent renovation has taken place since all of Jerusalem came under Israeli rule at the end of the 1967 War.

At the time of my husband's and my marriage ceremony, the four halls of worship were decorated in the architectural motifs of the Jews of Spain, Italy, and Turkey. The reds, blues, and greens of the stained glass windows complemented the off-white walls and gold-colored archways. This was the history of the synagogue where my husband and I were married. To us it was hallowed ground. When several years ago my daughter and I visited with my ex-husband, relatives, and friends in Jerusalem, the three of us stood on the very spot where our marriage chupah had been fourteen years earlier. Beautifully designed Sephardi-motif black wrought-iron fences and gates enclosed the area. The Torah scrolls were kept in carefully engraved cylindrical jackets of silver and gold colors, respectively. The designs were floral, with each container having a kind of crown at the top. A large Star of David was cut into the front of each Torah scroll encasement.

To get back to the wedding ceremony, all the people Simon and I had worked with from the Jewish National Fund and Hadassah Hospital were there, as well as Simon's immediate family. Unfortunately, only a few of my family were able to attend, as the train ride was nine hours either way from Nahariya, plus the additional travel to the synagogue, and we had no accommodations for them to sleep overnight. My friends, the Weisses, came, as well as Aunt Tsila and Uncle Yehiel, many rabbis whom Simon and I knew, with their spouses, and the Bnai Israel, Indian Jewish community. A group of Bnai Israel dancers could not come at the last minute, due to illness. Of course, our matchmakers, the Sidas, and their families were there. The synagogue was filled to capacity.

Simon and I gave the Ashkenazi caterer a bit of trouble with the menu, as we insisted on rice pallao covered with almonds and raisins, alongside of roast chicken, for which I carefully instructed the caterer. My future mother-in-law, future husband, and I decided on a Sephardi menu, and that it was. The caterer had never before cooked for a Sephardi Jewish wedding.

The first few months of our marriage were like the legendary Camelot. We enjoyed little things, like biting into either side of a peach together, going to the fabric market together to choose cloth for me to make quilts for the family, and visiting with friends and family. By coincidence (or was it destiny?) I had made my wedding gown in Simon's two favorite colors, silver lace on white polyester. It was interesting, how often we used to communicate by telepathy; one of us would think something and the other would reply. They say that it is a special gift of the spirit.

Simon and I often shopped together in East Jerusalem. In 1974 Jews and Arabs traded freely with each other. Also, the East Jerusalem Arabs profited appreciably from the tourist trade, especially the American tourists. Simon and I frequented several food and fabric shops, whose owners we got to know well and who gave us very good prices on items such as almonds and dates. These items do not cost much in America, but are very expensive in Israel, so getting them of good quality at bargain prices was a good deal. I got a kick out of one merchant there. When asked "How late do you keep open?" he answered, "Until I feel like closing." When asked what he charged for certain garments, he replied, "The price is right" or "Whatever I feel like charging," but he always gave us a decent price and made his comments in good humor.

The long, progressively descending stone pathways with short staircases of stone, covered by stone archways, were built many hundreds of years ago by the Crusaders. We learned to overlook the cows' and sheeps' heads hung outside the Arab butcher shops, along with other parts of the animals' carcasses, for sale. Again, for the benefit of Western tourists passing through these areas, this is the Oriental way of life. (In the heat of summer, one does worry about health problems, though.) One must keep in mind that Israel and its Arab-inhabited areas, such as East Jerusalem, Nazareth, Jericho, are part of the Middle East, as opposed to the Occident, or Western Hemisphere. Though Israel has its share of Westernization, following Western clothing fashions and using Western appliances, it is still primarily an Oriental country. I would not like to think of the day coming when the beautiful and diverse costumes of the Arabs and of the Jews and Jewesses of Tunisia, Yemen, and Ethiopia would suddenly become absorbed into a sea of Westernization. The number of Coke machines in a country does not determine its degree of civilization, but rather its respect for women, the aged, and education, and its care of the indigent.

As for the potential danger of my husband and I shopping in East Jerusalem, even back in 1974 there were occasional attacks by Arab terrorists there, but these were very rare. One did not go shopping there on a Friday, for if any pro-terrorist leader were to decide to incite Muslims to violence, it would most likely occur on that day, the day on which most mosque gatherings for services take place. As for religious regard in Israel, it is accepted that Jews close their businesses on Saturday, Muslims on Friday, and Christians on Sunday.

Regarding communication, most of the Arab merchants in East Jerusalem not only speak perfect Hebrew, but are also proficient in English, French, and Spanish. They are very multilingual people, and besides, it is important for their tourist businesses. I've learned barely enough Arabic to get by, though I understand more than I can speak. Before the advent of the shekel, the lira was used as Israeli currency. It is common for Arabs to try to spur up trade by calling, *"B'lira, b'lira,"* meaning "good prices." However, there is an extension of that expression, which is a vulgar term for the sex act. An Arab vendor said that to me once, at which I spat on the ground in front of him, held my head high, and walked on up the path. As I walked on, I heard a shopkeeper say in Arabic that I just managed to understand, "You just lost one of your best customers." Of course, my husband and I never did business with him again.

However, we got on fine with most of the vendors in East Jerusalem. I still have a finely hand-carved necklace of olive wood, purchased there. This painstaking art is a craft for which the Arab people are famous, and the workers sit for hours, cross-legged on the floor, in dimly lit rooms to produce such beautifully made items as earrings, belts, and animal figurines. I first learned of this jewelry in 1968, when Ulpan Etzion took all of us students on a tour of the country, including parts of the West Bank. We observed the wood carvers at work in Bethlehem at the time.

I have many other memories of shopping with my husband in both East and West Jerusalem, the best place to get bargains in the latter being in the Orthodox Jewish Mea Shaarim (hundred gates) section. In both places you always haggled. The vendors would think you had taken leave of your senses if you did not haggle. I have a silver incense burner, used to usher in the end of the Sabbath. Most cherished, though, is a miniature Torah scroll, about ten inches tall, encased in silver, which we bought from an Argentinian Jew (with whom I had a very pleasant conversation in Spanish).

As for our marriage, as luck would have it, Simon and I moved in with his mother, and were occasionally joined by my married brother-in-law, Eli. Strangely enough, Eli and his family never caused any of our marital problems, as one might expect the relatives with whom one lives to do. If anything, Eli tried to be a peacemaker. There is something to be said for living with in-laws. Members of an extended kinship family are often more supportive of one another, especially in times of grief or illness, than are members of the American-style husband, wife, and children family. Also, how very difficult it can be just to be a mother-in-law, trying to overlook or accept certain ideas of her children about love and raising a family. Some of these concepts may not only be foreign, but even anathema to a woman raised in a totally different culture, as were some of my concepts to my mother-in-law.

My mother-in-law, Hannah, had also lived through more than her share of bitter times. Though she and her husband, Joseph, had been accustomed to opulence and comfort and live-in servants when they lived in Rangoon, Burma, they were soon deprived of all of that when, during the Second World War, the Japanese bombed Rangoon. They literally had to drop everything, leaving behind many thousands of dollars worth of gold, silver, silks, and furniture. They then grabbed their children by the hands, with my brother-in-law Reuben still at my mother-in-law's breast, and ran for the harbor, through hundreds of bodies of fellow Burmese, the mangled dying mixed with the dead. The whole family barely made it through peltings of bombshells to the dock of a ship, into whose boiler room they made their way. They had no food or water whatever with them, and there they remained, vomiting, for five days and nights, till the ship reached Calcutta, India. There the Jews of Calcutta rescued them with tea, soup, and bread. Then the worst blow struck. After his bar mitzvah, Simon's brother, Mordecai, was suddenly stricken with dysentery and died. Whatever losses one may sustain in life, none can be more devastating than the loss of a child, especially one who is very kind and gifted, which everyone told me Mordecai was.

Shortly after that the family moved to Bombay, where they remained for the rest of the time they lived in India. They also had many cousins in Bombay and Calcutta, which made for a more close-knit family life for them. With the inauguration of the State of Israel, the Aarons, like so many other Indian Jews, decided to pack up all their worldly belongings and emigrate to Israel, in 1952. They first lived in a moshav of fellow Oriental Jews, Kfar Ofer, in the mountains near Haifa. A few years later they moved to Jerusalem, where they made their permanent home in Givat Shaul. There in the late 1960's my father-in-law, Joseph, passed away after a lengthy illness. I say my father-in-law, as from hearing of his goodness, even though he and I never met, I could feel his spiritual presence. All of the family and I visited his and the other family graves a few months before Ruth was born, and offered prayers for each one of them. I'm sure they heard us in heaven.

In addition, after I came to live with my husband and mother-in-law, she and I made the best of some of the hard times during the Yom Kippur War. For example, the potatoes that were available for general consumption were cold-storage ones, while the fresh fruit and vegetables, as well as meat, were saved primarily for the wounded and sick soldiers on the front. Thus, Mummy (which my mother-in-law had me and the other sons- and daughters-in-law call her) and I spent a good part of the time digging big, black, dead worms out of the cold-storage potatoes, as well as picking out the tiny, live, white worms from the beets, in order to prepare an Indian soup called *cuttah* (made with beets and beet greens, tomatoes, onions, garlic, chicken, potatoes, lemon and spices). Though my mother-in-law and I did not see "eye-to-eye" about many matters, yet I learned a great deal from her. We also empathized with each other about the hardships we all went through as a family, living in a wartime situation.

I remember the day, when I was about six months pregnant and had gone shopping for chicken and vegetables in the Mahane Yehuda shuk, that I returned home an hour late, apologizing, "I'm sorry I'm an hour late, Mummy. A bomb just blew up in front of me." Her expression showed that she was genuinely concerned about me, and glad that I had come home alive. Actually, I was quite fortunate that day, as Simon and I were on several other occasions.

On one such occasion the PLO had planted a bomb inside an egg crate, a place that no one would have suspected, alongside of the niche where an old Israeli sat, selling shoelaces and other sundry items, and in front of a bakery on the corner of the street. As I walked up the street from the post office, where intuition had told me to go first to buy aerogrammes, suddenly the bomb exploded, blasting a hole through the bakery, which sent pieces of buns, shtrudel, and broken glass flying all over the place. The lady proprietor of the bakery was pinned against the pastry display window, where fragments of glass had hit her on either side of the neck, the blood streaming down her neck onto her dress and shoulders. Thank heavens, the wounds were not serious, and she was able to be treated at the Shaare Zedek Hospital and then released. The shoelace vendor went into cardiac arrhythmia, for which he also was treated at the hospital and then released. Other passers-by were moderately wounded. We were extremely fortunate that no life was lost in this case. The proprietor of the bakery remained badly shaken for a few days, but then returned to work. Such terrorist bombings were not uncommon then, especially in Jerusalem.

The Israeli bomb squad was on the scene almost within moments, and made a full investigation into the matter, as well as helping the wounded. As the damage had already been done, and all the rescue squads were immediately on the scene, I decided that I might as well go on with the shopping I had originally planned. Our butcher said that the Almighty must have been watching over me, as this was the third occasion during which I was at Mahane Yehuda when terrorist bombs went off, and I was not harmed. That really made me count my blessings. Once having purchased the chicken and vegetables we needed, I left the shuk as quickly as possible and headed for home, where as I already stated, my mother-in-law greeted me, holding her breath.

Aside from those aspects of our lives, though my husband was very kind and selfless, and I tried to fit into the household, the combination of our faults plus living with his mother proved unbearable. Five months after our baby was on the way, our marriage was crumbling. Both my husband and I had made serious mistakes. Thus, after we had been married about two years, Simon and I got divorced.

The most important thing for a newly wed couple, besides compromising and compensating, is to hold off on conceiving children until six months to a year after the wedding. That gem of advice I got from Dr. Nicholas Fiumara, one of our best lecturers in nursing school. That way, no possibly unwanted child is thrust into a situation of unhappiness and instability.

The divorce in and of itself does not need to be that traumatic, if there is not real love between the two marriage partners. However, in our case, it was very traumatic, because Simon and I really loved each other. Nevertheless, a marriage cannot thrive on love alone. One person to whom I am indebted for supporting me through this awful time was a friend named Sujata Whaley, whom I had met years before in America, and who became as a sister to me. When Sujata and I first met, she was still married to her American husband (Sujata had originally come from the south of India), and many were the delightful occasions when she and I, dressed in the finery of our sarees, attended the dinners and dance festivals of the India Society of Greater Boston. We also visited with each other and slept over at each other's homes, along with Sujata's pet German shepherd named Naio, which meant Daisy in Polynesian. Sujata also taught me how to cook delicious *dahl* (a thick, soupy dish made of various lentils, with slivered garlic, onion, tomatoes, and Indian spices). Sujata's marriage was soon, unfortunately, also to end in divorce, which gave her the insight, from her own painful experience, to counsel me by letters to Jerusalem, when Simon's and my marriage started to go on the rocks.

I felt so alone and shattered by the prospect of my divorce from Simon that I fell into a rut of depression. Then I wrote of this to Sujata, and she, in turn, sent me letters, full of understanding and compassion. She told me to try to concentrate only on the relationship between Simon and me, leaving his mother and her feelings out as much as possible. She imparted to me a strength from within that I would not otherwise have been able to muster on my own. After the baby and I returned to America, Sujata never considered it too much to baby-sit, even all day, gratis, for little Ruth (that was my daughter's birth name, which she changed to Dalya at age seventeen), while I dashed out to do some shopping. We spent Passover together, too, which made it all the more meaningful. As a librarian, Sujata was well educated about Judaism, as well as other religions, and had great respect for my faith. She had also been very dedicated to Mama

Tzipah, visiting her often while I was in Israel, in addition to caring for her parents, making frequent trips to England to look after them. About ten years ago, Dalya and I spent Passover with Sujata, with Sujata being able to enjoy her adopted niece, now quite grown up. She will always be in my heart.

TWELVE

JUDAIC AND CHRISTIAN ISSUES

To return to the previously mentioned subject of Jewish-Christian relationships, I have been impressed by a variety of attitudes demonstrated by Christian people among whom I was raised. One whose memory will always be sacred to me was a man I called Uncle Ralph. His full name was Ralph Taylor Hensey. He was an African-American Christian who saved my grandmother, mother, and me from freezing when I was four years old. A friend of the family, Gerty Goldman, on hearing of our plight, rushed to our house to tell Mama Tzipah that she knew of a very kind-hearted man who worked at Bloomberg's furniture store and was an expert at repairing stoves. Mama gratefully accepted Gerty's offer to seek out the man and ask him to help us. About a half-hour later Gerty returned with a tall, lanky, well-built man, wearing glasses, who had a compassionate smile on his dark brown face. Ralph came to our house in a bitter winter frost, descended into the cellar, and worked steadfastly away at the stove for hours, carrying gallons of oil up the stairs, until he got our oil burner working.

Having two young daughters of his own, Uncle Ralph easily picked me up and put me on his shoulders for a ride up and down the cellar stairs, which I shyly accepted. Mama then invited him to stay for coffee and homemade cookies, and we all sat down to a pleasant conversation together. We were quite poor then, and Mama had only one dollar, which she gave Ralph with much gratitude. I had a severe chest infection at the time, from which, thanks to Uncle Ralph, I recovered quickly. Later, when Mama went to look for the mail, she found the dollar bill, which Uncle Ralph had returned. From that day on our families "adopted" each other, and Uncle Ralph adopted me as his little niece.

Many were the pleasant days that Uncle Ralph visited with Mama Tzipah and me, with me perched on his knee, and he and Mama discussing each other's families, proper raising of children, politics, and helping the needy of the world. These conversations were always accompanied by generous servings of Mama's homemade shtrudel or mandelbread (Eastern European Jewish pastry delicacies made of nuts, raisins, and cinnamon) and many cups of percolated coffee. I really think that the United Nations should have included Mama Tzipah and Uncle Ralph in their General Assembly sessions, as they arrived at more solutions to the social and political ills of the world than do most other people.

Uncle Ralph set more than an example of simple kindness for me, though. He was a master craftsman of the highest order, taking great pride and care in every television, refrigerator, or stove that he repaired. If an appliance was not worth repairing, he would tell the customer directly not to waste his money on it—this in an age when "big bucks" for the sake of gain itself was becoming common practice. Perhaps that was why Uncle Ralph never became wealthy, as other appliance repairmen did. He had integrity of a unique sort, and would rather go home with less money than cheat people.

When years later I dated a man who was in the appliance repair business, and he told me that he would "repair" a washing machine that a child had dropped a wooden block into the back of, "to make the business come in," I was provoked at his low code of ethics. I told him I couldn't accept that, and refused to see him again. I had no need of a man with less integrity than my Uncle Ralph's.

When, on the occasion of our graduation from nursing school, Uncle Ralph and Aunt Hazel's older daughter, Gloria, suddenly died after undergoing surgery, I attended the funeral, of course, as did many other friends and family members. I felt bitter when the nursing school housemother reproached me for not going to the post-graduation lunch with the other girls. I couldn't even dignify her comment with a response, as the last thing on my mind was merry-making, after Gloria's funeral. Did she think it inappropriate because Gloria's skin was black and mine was white? She was as family to me, and I felt sorry for the housemother, if this was the extent of her insight and compassion.

A couple of years after that, I invited Uncle Ralph and Aunt Hazel to my new apartment for a dinner of spaghetti and meatballs, tossed salad, wine, coffee, homemade mandelbread, and fruit salad. We talked about family matters and my new nursing career, told jokes, and then played classical music on my record player. Just as they were leaving, I wrapped some of the mandelbread in tin foil for Uncle Ralph and Aunt Hazel to take home. At that we hugged and kissed each other good-bye, and Uncle Ralph commented about the mandelbread: "Sandy, you're your grandmother's child, sending us home with pastry." It was the last dinner we would have together. Aunt Hazel died of a heart attack shortly after that, to add to Uncle Ralph's grief. Only his other daughter, Joan, and her husband and children, plus another brother, Elwood (who was to die soon after that), his aging mother, and I remained. Uncle Ralph deserved far better than that out of life. Religious people say that we're not supposed to ask questions about such things, but I still do.

G-d took Uncle Ralph from us in the summer of 1987, after suffering from cancer. Like unto him, so beautiful of soul, there are few in existence. Uncle Ralph died with his second wife, Jean, at his side, as she had cared for him steadfastly throughout his final illness. I shall never forgive myself for not having stayed with Uncle Ralph till his last moments, as I had to be on duty that night in neurosurgery, and only remained with his hand in mine till about two-o'clock that afternoon. His breathing was labored, so that he was no longer able to speak, but could still understand what was said to him. Before I left, I reiterated to him that Ruth (Dalya had not yet changed her name) and I loved him very much and always would, and that he would be given the full honor he deserved in the book that I was attempting to publish. Cousin Carol called me just as I was about to go to sleep in preparation for the night shift, to tell me that Uncle Ralph had just died, with minimal suffering. It was about three-thirty in the afternoon.

However, not all gentiles, in the United States in particular, have had the same broad-minded attitude as my late Uncle Ralph. This was best expressed by Dr. Franklin H. Littell, former president of Iowa-Wesleyan College and then professor of religion at Temple University, in his book *Wild Tongues,* in which he refers to the cultural anti-Semitism that infects "Christian America." He states: "The truth is that the 'Founding Fathers' neither intended nor erected a high wall of separation between church and state. Nor did they establish a Christian nation, for basic religious commitment is not subject to legislation. We are moving forward, in American history, to strengthen voluntary religion."[1]

Again I wish to quote Dr. Littell: "The believing Christian will pray for his persecuted brethren in Communist or fascist or Muslim territory. . . . he will pray that dictators will be brought low and liberty flourish; he will not, however, if his mind and spirit are shaped by the G-d of the Bible, make a superficial identification of national and ethnic interests with Christianity. He will not preach a holy war of "Christian America" against "atheistic Russia" and "Red China." Dr. Littell further states: "Racist ideology is a two-edged sword, and, whether white or black, it represents a betrayal of high religion and also of the American dream."[2]

I remember well the times when other Jewish children and I were attacked and beaten in Chelsea by Christian youths who shouted, "You Jews killed our Saviour." The overall American attitude since that time does not seem very much improved, especially at Christmas time, and especially as far as charity is concerned. I could not help but feel disgusted as I saw countless shoppers jamming the department stores during a recent December, buying their children hundred-dollar trains and eighty-dollar game sets. Others were buying their spouses garments for hundreds of dollars each, but not one of them gave money to the man from the Salvation Army, nor did they give one dime when people representing the homeless asked them for a donation. I overheard one man as he recounted his gifts and commented, "I wouldn't give a damned thing to help those homeless bums—they wouldn't appreciate it, anyway."

I personally happen to have known many of those people he referred to as "homeless bums" and know for a fact that they often are living in shelters or in public parks because their factories folded. They couldn't be trained for new occupations soon enough, were refused others, went broke, and were evicted from their homes for lack of funds to pay rent. Boston alone lays claim to over five thousand such people, many of whom would be immensely grateful for any job to maintain their dignity. We are going through a depression now somewhat like the one our country saw in the 1930's.

I did not see any of those busy shoppers who were stocking up on expensive wines, fruits, and meats offer to help any of their fellow Americans who were hungry, or volunteer to give a donation to Helen Keller International, which provides malnourished children overseas with Vitamin A supplements to prevent them from going blind from xeropthalmia. I doubt that they gave to the United Nations Save the Children Fund either. One well-to-do patient I cared for said to me, "There will always be the poor anyway." This is true, but it does not mean we should do nothing to help some of the poor out of their poverty.

If there is an example of caring, it has been set by Mother Teresa and her Order's Missionaries of Charity, who care for "the poorest of the poor" and the dying in Calcutta, India, and in other parts of the world where Mother Teresa established branches of the Order. It would behoove many who consider themselves good Christians to learn from the late Mother Teresa and her Sisters. They could learn from Mother Teresa's bathing people who have been eaten by worms, and those who are almost too grim to behold, as the Sisters of Charity feed and comfort them. Let the "good Christians" learn to emulate these acts of charity, for it is written in Corinthians (in the New Testament) that among acts of goodness, charity ranks the highest of them all.

If there is a true love of humanity, it has been exhibited by the late Dr. Thomas A. Morris, Jr., and his wife, who took care of nearly thirty foster children for many years. They did it for the sheer joy of loving children who would otherwise have fallen into the category of "unwanted children." These children's lives were filled with love and enrichment. This the Morrises did in addition to caring for their own children.

There is love requiring nothing in return in the person of Judge Joseph L. Tauro, who for many years has given of himself, far and above the call of duty, to the mentally retarded of Massachusetts. The impact of his work has extended far beyond this state alone. It has been a thankless job, fraught with material hardships and severely frustrating political barriers, to get the necessary funds, housing facilities, and proper staff to administer to a helpless group who need total physical care and a great deal of kindness. No sum of money would be enough to repay Judge Tauro's selflessness and dedication.

As for Judaeo-Christian dialogue, there are certain basic misunderstandings about Judaism that have needed to be corrected. Many people believe that Jewish doctors and nurses will not care for a sick person on the Sabbath. This is untrue. The breaking of the Sabbath, or even Yom Kippur, the holiest of holy days, is permitted for the saving of lives or the redemption of captives. This means that if there are insufficient gentiles to alternate with Jewish medical personnel on holy days, then Jews may care for the sick, with honor.

The primitive fantasies that Christianity has for centuries cruelly sustained were sadistically brought forth in 1543 in the pamphlet "On the Jews and Their Lives" by Martin Luther, founder of the Protestant Reformation. This pamphlet resulted, indirectly, in the Nazi Holocaust some four hundred years later. It contributed to centuries of ignorance and falsity that culminated in the worst, most massive genocide in history. Here is some of what was in the pamphlet: "They [the Jews] have been . . . murderers of all Christendom for more than fourteen hundred years in their kidnapping of children, of piercing them through with an awl, of hacking them in pieces. . . . The sun has never shone on a more bloodthirsty and vengeful people." The exact method of how to perform the genocide follows here: "First set fire to their synagogues or schools. . . . Second, I advise that their houses also be razed and destroyed. . . . Third, I advise that all their prayer books be taken from them. . . . Fourth, I advise that their rabbis be forbidden to teach henceforth on pain of loss of life and limb. . . . We must drive them out like mad dogs. . . . I have done my duty. Now let everyone see to his."[3]

In 1874, Adolph Stoecker of the church of Berlin, stated, "The Jews are Germany's misfortune."[4] Sixty years later Hitler repeated this statement verbatim and ordered all of the steps to rid Germany of its Jews according to the treatise of Martin Luther of 1543. This background is relevant to the attack on my grandmother and her other blind friends in 1968 in Roxbury, earlier described, as well as to the false bases of all anti-Semitism. This had occurred during the period of time (1960's through early 1970's) known as the "Reign of Terror," when African-American militants struck the Boston area, hitting the Jewish community in particular, attacking Jews, burning synagogues and Sifrei Torah.

There is, however, far more than meets the eye in this situation. The Ashkenazi Jews, who comprised the bulk of the population of Roxbury and Dorchester, had begun moving out in droves when the first African-American families moved into the area. It was a repeat performance of what had happened in Harlem, New York. In Boston, in particular, this could not have been less justified. The first African-American family to buy a house on Sonoma Street were a model American family, the husband being an engineer and his wife a dress designer. Their two children were very well mannered. This was in 1955, if memory serves me correctly. We shall call this family the Porters.

When they first moved into the community, they put themselves at great expense, throwing a strictly kosher catered party to which they invited all the Jewish neighbors of the area. Mr. Porter told them all, "We don't want this to become another Harlem. We want to live in peace and harmony with you all, and we don't want anyone leaving because of us.

Nonetheless, within two weeks two Jewish families had sold their homes on that street for half the price they were worth, to two African-American families from the Deep South. This was much to the chagrin of the Porters and everyone else in the area. That anyone should move out of an area because of someone else's color is irrational. There was not one sensible reason for the above two families to sell their property.

In contrast, as is commonly known, if destructive, lawless elements move into an area, it is difficult to prevent it from declining, which is what eventually happened in Roxbury and Dorchester. Notwithstanding, the rest of the Jewish community could have rallied, together with the Porters and other concerned residents, to prevent the area from being invaded by undesirables. There was one bastion of strength in the area at that time, in the form of the Jewish Defense League, led by the brilliant and energetic Rabbi Marvin Antelman. Although, according to Hillel Levine and Lawrence Harmon in their book *The Death of an American Jewish Community*, some considered the rabbi an agitator as he went about with his group of Jewish followers defending the Jews of Blue Hill Avenue, it was because of the fearlessness and dedication of this man that many other young Jewish men joined in the protection of harassed Jewish women and elders. Rabbi Antelman also went forward with the blessing of Grand Rabbi Levi I. Horowitz, who instructed the members of his Brookline congregation to support Rabbi Antelman. Among the rabbi's followers was Arthur Bernstein of the Jewish Community Council, much to the chagrin of other J.C.C. leaders.[5]

Perhaps if the Greater Boston Jewish establishment had supported Rabbi Antelman and his hundred and fifty followers, the beautiful, tree-lined Blue Hill Avenue, with its florist shops, Jewish bakeries, Jewish butcher shops, Hebrew bookstores (especially Davidson's Hebrew Bookstore, which sold all manner of Hebrew and Yiddish religious and historical articles), and delicatessens, to mention only a few, might never have been vandalized, robbed, and reduced to rubble. Perhaps if the Jewish establishment had supported Rabbi Antelman and the Jewish Defense League, the *shtiblech* (home synagogues) and elegant two- and three-story wooden houses in Washington Park and on Woodrow Avenue, Savannah Avenue, Seaver Street, and Humboldt Avenue, many with trellised gardens and flower-decorated front porches, would never have been broken into, vandalized, and burned. Perhaps if Rabbi Antelman had been supported, African-American militants would never have burned the Agudas Israel synagogue and the Chevra Shas synagogue with its Sifrei Torah in May of 1970.[5]

For us as Jews, the burning of a Sefrei Torah is considered the worst sacrilege. I remember attending the funeral of the Sifrei Torah of the Chevra Shas synagogue, in the company of well over a thousand fellow Jews. It was one of the saddest occasions of the entire Greater Boston Jewish community, and essentially signified the collapse of the Jewish community of Roxbury and Dorchester. Among the rabbis who gave the eulogies for the Sifrei Torah, I felt that the most meaningful by far was that given by the Grand Rabbi Levi I. Horowitz. Besides stating the total dejection felt by all Jews at this most blasphemous of desecrations, the Bostonner Rebbe (as the Grand Rabbi is affectionately called by all local Jews) also stated that such an act of anti-Semitic desecration must not be allowed to go unmentioned and unpunished by the gentile Boston community. He said that this unpardonable destruction of all that is holy to Judaism, embodied the hearts and souls of the Hebrew people.

It was, he stated, the rekindling of the Nazi Holocaust, where during Kristallnacht, the Night of the Broken Glass, thousands of Hebrew Bibles, holy books, and Sifrei Torah were put to torch.

As for what else Rabbi Antelman might have salvaged, from my childhood up to age twelve I remember the Chanukkah and Purim parties we celebrated at the Seaver Street Young Men's and Women's Hebrew Association, in the huge, beautifully decorated auditorium. White and blue crepe paper streamers were strung up across the ceiling, with gold metallic drapes with Stars of David covering the walls. The costumed children (wearing Maccabee, Hebrew soldiers' costumes) sang Chanukah songs in Hebrew and English, and the adults joined the children for Hebrew dances. Of course, at the Chanukkah parties *soovganiot* (donuts) were served to all, with punch. At the Purim parties the children and adults masqueraded as Queen Esther, her Uncle Mordecai, or King Ahashueros. Hamantashen and kosher grape juice were served to all.

For me, the most outstanding holiday was Simchat Torah, the celebration of G-d's giving us the holy laws, as it was celebrated inside the Chai Odom synagogue, and outside on Intervale Street. In the middle of the street the men, all dressed in suits and wearing hats, with small children sitting on their shoulders, danced around in a circle, singing Torah songs, with the women and girls forming a separate circle. In the center were Jews holding high the Sifrei Torah. It was the most heartwarming sight. Regrettably, it will never be seen again in Roxbury or Dorchester.

It is interesting to note what can be achieved when a group of concerned citizens band together to guard their area, unlike the above situation. This was done most effectively by the Italian-Americans in Boston's North End, at about the same time the difficulties began in Roxbury and Dorchester. A couple of African-American thugs decided to harass a lemonade and hot dog vendor on Salem Street with switchblade knives. A distress signal was sounded, and within minutes every able-bodied Italian-American male rallied to the side of his neighbors and the attack was squelched before it could gain any headway. If the thugs had brought reinforcements, they could have outnumbered the Italians five to one, but the Italian-Americans had such strength of unity that the thugs, badly beaten, left and never returned.

The Chinese-Americans likewise band together for mutual defense, as they have shown in a number of recent situations in Boston's Chinatown, and they do so very effectively. They have been buying out an adjacent area known as the "combat zone" (consisting of strip-tease, drug, and alcohol establishments that have created problems for Chinatown) and have been turning the area into a Chinese cultural and mercantile district. When a Chinese man was recently accused falsely of soliciting a prostitute and was beaten by a Boston police officer, concerned Chinese-Americans, as well as witnesses to the scene, came to Mr. Fung's defense and won the case for him. It is very regrettable that the Jews of America have not yet learned to stand up similarly for their own.

Aside from the issue of self-defense, there must be no higher priority than education, and without Jewish leadership pouring more money into the Yeshivot, they are beginning to dwindle. The centers of all Hebrew culture and education are the Yeshivot, and the Jewish community ceases to properly exist without their tutelage. This is true especially in light of the recent impetus toward Reformed Judaism and intermarriage. That means that the full meaning of Halacha (the written law, already described) and Haggada (Hebrew history and ethics), both comprising Talmud, are passed over lightly, and the bases of Jewish belief are lost.

Contrary to what some people say, the written law and kashruth are not anachronisms. They are the basis of a profound code of ethics, as well as cleanliness, and extend into every aspect of Jewish life, thus avoiding many forms of animal-borne diseases. Also, Halacha can be amended by order of a rabbinical concourse, but not changed, as some Jews wish to change the Jewish lineage to be based on the father's as well as the mother's blood line. This cannot be allowed, for therein begins the destruction by assimilation (through intermarriage or mixed marriages) of the Hebrew people.

Also, the direction of Jewish funds to most non-Jewish organizations and causes drains the needed funds away from the aforementioned institutions. There is nothing worse than the false generosity that patronizes groups with questionable leanings because it is the politically advantageous thing to do. We need to help Jews locally, as well as throughout the world, with emigration to Israel, housing, Yeshivot, and health care services. We also need to provide Sifrei Torah in places where our people haven't any.

The Greater Boston Jewish leadership, as it stands now, neither provides for adequate Yeshiva funding nor helps Jews adequately to get jobs. It is a sad state of affairs when local Jewish agencies employ many people from other minority groups, but few of their own. I had an interesting conversation not long ago with an African-American city councilor who told me, "I make it a point to find qualified Black people to give jobs to before I consider anyone else." I give that man credit in that he helps his own before he helps others. It is appalling that the one Jewish hospital in Boston no longer has a kosher kitchen. A number of non-observant Jews have commented, "For those patients who want strictly kosher meals, they can always have the hospital order it." The principle goes beyond that though. Any observant Jewish family who visit with a patient should be able to buy kosher food in the cafeteria. The primary help given at such an institution should also be directed to the needy of the Jewish community before giving it to others.

Likewise, when Jews are being discriminated against in employment and housing, it should be the business of the Jewish establishment to intervene and apply pressure to existing local, state, and federal agencies that deal with discrimination to assist the Jews involved. They should also provide legal assistance on a sliding scale for that purpose, so that those who can afford to pay would do so, and those who cannot would not be humiliated because of indigency. The *yishuv* (Jewish community, originally of Israel) of America must provide its own form of "affirmative action" agency. Also, counseling in regard to vocational rehabilitation and job finding for local Jews should be enhanced. The majority of American Jews are in the middle and lower middle classes, economically. It is they who should be helped by the well-to-do Jewish establishment.

The problem with most of the preceding situations is that the Jewish establishment would have to confront institutions that are denying local Jews employment or housing, and to confront certain other minority groups who are harassing or causing other problems for the Jews. The Italian-Americans, Chinese-Americans, and African-Americans do not hesitate to confront when one of theirs has been wronged; Jews should not fear to confront in defense of their own people. One Jewish lawyer told me a long time ago, "It's not considered politically advisable for Jews to confront another minority group." Therefore, the injustices continue unchallenged.

To confront means to stand out alone and risk ostracism. It means trying to effect changes for the betterment of one's fellow human beings that may entail personal hurt, castigation, and sometimes loss of friends. It means risking rejection by the establishment, possible loss of social and/ or political status, and sometimes loss of one's job. If the injustices are great enough, and the need of rectification imperative, then we have to weigh the possible cost of confrontation against the moral obligations we have to individuals who have been wronged.

The former Senator Margaret Chase Smith, Louis Brandeis, President John F. Kennedy and his brother Robert, and Reverend Dr. Martin Luther King, Jr., confronted in the name of humanity and dignity, and unfortunately the last three paid for it with their lives. However, their lives and deaths were not in vain. They effected changes from which Jews, African-Americans, and all oppressed people have benefited. They did it without violence, but with relentless demonstrations and publicity to let the world know that they would not allow human oppression. Dr. King did this in a highly organized fashion, against severe odds of bigotry in his marches in Montgomery, Alabama, and elsewhere. They all followed in the footsteps of the Mahatma Gandhi, whose great, nonviolent leadership ultimately achieved India's independence from Great Britain. It also helped to outlaw the demeaning caste system in India. As we know from history, the Mahatma was also unfortunately murdered by a fanatic. However, his soul still leads all the conscientious confronters of the world to strive for justice.

This is what the Jews of America must do. It may mean Jewish lawyers giving some of their time gratis to help fellow Jews. It may also mean vigilant groups of Jews (not illegally armed thugs) standing guard at Jewish institutions to quell anti-Semitic disturbances. Women as well as men trained in the martial arts can participate in such patrols, as I personally have done in the company of fellow Jews. These patrols have in the past proved to be a strong deterrent against vandals, hoodlums, and anti-Semites.

It may also mean Jewish housewives and daughters staying up late on occasion, packing sandwiches for the vigilantes who go out on patrols. It may include Jewish community meetings to decide which institutions need help the most, and how it should be given. It may also necessitate the Jewish leadership going out into the community and confronting acts of anti-Semitism on college campuses and at other places. In the broader sense it means helping those of our people in lands where they are being persecuted, such as Iran, Syria, and Argentina.

For about a decade, the late Rabbi Meir Kahane, former national leader of the Jewish Defense League in the United States, became the strongest activist leader of the Kach (Thus) political party, which essentially advocates Israel for the Jews, more or less exclusively (which is not my personal opinion). The Jews of America needed him much more desperately here, in the United States. Tsahal, the Israeli Defense Forces, adequately defend Israel. What the Jews of America need now is a powerful, outspoken leader and self-defense organizer like the late Rabbi Kahane, with the intestinal fortitude to stand up to the anti-Semitic groups currently plaguing the United States. As we know, the noble Rabbi Kahane was gunned down while giving a lecture in New York City on November 5, 1990. Rabbi Antelman and his family now live in Israel, following a lawsuit brought against him by the late anti-Semitic community activist, Elma Lewis.

THIRTEEN

INDIA

A WORD NEEDS TO BE SAID AT THIS POINT ABOUT THE MUTUAL BACKGROUNDS MY EX-HUSBAND AND I SHARED. He and his family had spent over fifteen years in India, primarily in Calcutta and Bombay (which in the 1940's had large Jewish populations) after fleeing the Japanese bombings of Rangoon, Burma. At one time the Nagpada section of Bombay claimed twenty thousand Jews and the oldest synagogue in India, Shaar HaRachamim, or the Gates of Mercy. It was built by a Jew named Shmuel Yeheskel Divekar as a tribute to G-d for the Mogul Emperor's setting him free several centuries ago, during the military takeover of India by the Emperor. I regrettably spent only a month visiting with friends in India in 1971, in the Punjab (which means Land of Five Rivers in Hindi). I wish I could have stayed a year, but the cheap round-trip plane ticket I had was good only for a month.

Notwithstanding the extreme contrast between Western living as I knew it and Indian life, I found the people of India rich with culture, religion, and most of all, family caring. It is a fact of life that in India there are nursing homes only for Brahman cows. (It is considered profane to kill them.) A relative will care for you if you should become widowed, ill, or old. Even a distant cousin will offer hospitality to a kinsman in dire straits. It may be only a bowl of rice and dahl, but they are shared freely. There is no such thing as turning out one's elders because they are no longer useful or have become senile or bedridden. In the Indian extended kinship household, all pitch in for the care of the elderly. Family relationships are not always ideal, but they reach a higher standard than most of ours in the United States. In the Indian household there is almost always a relative to whom one can turn regarding problems of health, finances, or quarrels, for advice and comfort.

It is so heartwarming to see bus drivers stop to allow time for a daughter-in-law or grandchild to bend over to touch the feet of an elder, as a sign of respect for their age and wisdom. Also, indecent assaults on women are rare in India, as there is much respect for the chastity of women. Unfortunately, there is limited freedom of thought for women. Marriages are often arranged, and large families, especially those with many sons (as is also the tenet of thought among Arabs), are considered a blessing. The role of most women in India at that time I was there was traditional, that is, at home, and as a rule mostly men were considered fit to enter the professions. I did, however, meet some Indian women who were bankers, journalists, computer engineers, and doctors. As a woman of Middle Eastern heritage, I knew of the strong preference of Middle Eastern and Indian women for a female gynecologist or obstetrician to provide their care. Thus there are many female Indian gynecologists and obstetricians who are at least as well qualified as their male Western counterparts. Dr. Uppal, about whom I shall presently write in more detail, was one such female physician. The Vellore Nursing School, in Vellore, India, also had a very high standard of nursing education, preparing women for another much-needed profession. At the turn of the twenty-first century, it is my understanding that Indian women are well-represented in many other scientific and technical fields, such as computer engineering.

It is heart-rending to see the suffering of the *achut,* or untouchables (those without caste). The Mahatma Gandhi referred to them as "the beloved of G-d" in his newspaper, the *Harijan,* which is the other Hindustani name for the untouchables. Though the caste system was outlawed in India several decades ago, in practice it still exists in many communities, to the point that many people will not marry out of their caste. I learned to take it very seriously when I was shown newspaper advertisements in which families indicated that they wished to arrange a marriage for their son or daughter. For example, an ad might read, "Family seeking for marriage with our daughter a man of Kshatriya caste (warrior's caste), professionally employed, in age range of thirties, and with good familial references. Please write Shrimati Nanduri at P.O. Box 458, Bombay." Such ads are taken very seriously in India, and are not done as jokes. When the person responds to the ad, both families' integrity is very carefully checked out.

The day of my arrival in India held a number of enlightenments and shocks. First, we had to change planes at Bombay airport to get to Palam airport in New Delhi. We were supposed to wait an hour for the transit plane, but after the first hour an announcer called out on the loud speaker, "There will be a temporary delay in the plane for New Delhi. We shall keep you informed. Thank you." Three more such announcements were made, two hours apart, the last one stating, "The plane for New Delhi will be leaving very immediately. Thank you for your cooperation and patience." From the time of landing at Bombay airport, "very immediately" ended up being eight hours later. There were no magazines to read in the meantime, nor had I brought a good book or knitting to occupy my time. We were free to order some snacks at the airport café, which seemed to consist of grayish beige tables, walls, floors, and waiters' uniforms all blended into one. Also, at one point a holy man, or guru, appeared on the spot, and hundreds of his followers suddenly charged in, almost squashing the rest of us in the process. In the meantime, I exchanged some small conversation with a well-to-do middle-aged Indian couple who thought rather ill of poor people, stating, "The poor don't know what to do with themselves." I did not reply to that.

When finally we reached New Delhi, Sudarshan, my friend from Boston, and her cousin, Inderjit, were awaiting me there, to my great joy. The inner part of the Palam airport was ultra-modern, so I faced a total culture shock as we exited and took a cab to Inderjit's house, seeing en route hundreds of men, women, and children squatting to use the gutters along the roadside as public toilets, covering themselves for modesty. Most of the buildings we passed appeared to have been built in the eighteenth century, of the same grayish beige material we had seen in the Bombay airport. The roads were not fully paved, and the bumps added to the exhaustion and indigestion I had already acquired during the long trip. I believe I am not really suited to long airplane trips, this one having been, stops included, forty-eight hours.

I shall always remember the love of Kamala Vati, my Punjabi Mama-ji, and Kanta, Inderjit's wife, at whose home Sudarshan, my "honorary sister," and I spent the first few days after arriving at New Delhi. Despite the language barrier (I spoke no Hindi and Kanta spoke no English), I was made to feel very much at home by Kanta. She and Inderjit have three children, who were the epitome of politeness. Though I felt somewhat as if I were a guest at a mortuary, what with the stone slab I was given to sleep on, Kanta's kindness made up for it. It took a bit of adjusting for her and her neighbors to understand why these strange Americans do not like their food cooked with lots of red-hot chilis (I thought my throat would burn up!). Going to the toilet was quite an experience, as we had to put each foot on a large, slippery stone cut into the shape of a foot, with a large hole in the floor, in a semi-squatting position, to relieve ourselves. You poured a bucket of water down the hole after washing yourself down below. The toilets were typically in a small stone house apart from the living quarters. There were few separate, closed sewage systems in India at that time. Since 1971, the year of my visit, India has made considerable progress in modernizing such systems, although the more primitive living conditions still persist in many urban and rural areas.

Kanta took Sudarshan and me to the local bazaar, where all manner of fabrics, pottery, sandals, and household items were sold. One always bargains, of course, at a bazaar. On a similar expedition in Jullundur later, I not only had several lovely Punjabi "pantsuits," consisting of a *shalwar camise* (tunic) and *shooridas* (women's trousers), made for me by the family tailor, but also bought half a dozen exquisitely embroidered silk sarees and gold earrings for myself. Of course, I bought gifts for the family back home in the United States, too. In India, as a rule, you do not just buy jewelry. You have the particular earrings and necklaces made to order of pure gold by the family goldsmith, who will have inherited this trade from his father, and his father's father before him. These crafts are a matter of family pride and tradition in India.

I made the stupid mistake of walking into the jeweler's with my sandals on, and I was quickly corrected. One does not bring soil from the street into the house or shop in India. Also, the streets in most of India had no sidewalk, with a rough kind of cobblestone extending from one side of the narrow streets to the other. Many of the shops consisted of one dimly lit room, into which all the wares, customers, shopkeepers, and employees were crammed. The workers sat cross-legged in the Oriental sitting position on mats on the floor, and did their stitching there. I thought it was touching to see one young male apprentice spontaneously offer a young mother nursing her baby a crate to sit on. All mothers breast-feed in India, with no one paying any particular attention to them, in private or in public, as it should be.

After Kanta's kind hospitality for several days, it came time for Sudarshan and me to make the day-long train trip to her home in Jullundur. Though Sudarshan did her best to keep up my spirits, it was a very draining trip, trying to acclimate myself to the Indian-style toilets (previously described, the only difference being that the opening in the train floor was directly over the train tracks), as well as the red-hot spicy food served as snacks, with extremely strong tea to wash it down. The view from the windows of the train made me think of centuries gone by, with water buffalos pulling primitive ploughs to till the fields, with the farmer or his wife prodding the animal along with a stick.

After this grueling ride, it was such a relief to be greeted that night by Sudarshan's mother, Kamala Vati, and her family, as she tenderly embraced me, and seeing my exhaustion, gently put my head on her lap and held me there, as she ordered the carriage driver to return to their bungalow. Despite her being about eighty pounds overweight, Kamala Vati was a very beautiful lady, with a round face, arched eyebrows over lovely dark eyes, a well-formed nose, and perfect lips. Her long hair was pulled back into a pug and covered by a saree, deftly drawn over her head. Only her daughter Madhu resembled her. All her other children, including Sudarshan, resembled the father, with slightly full lips and green eyes. Sudarshan was the most attractive, with her long jet-black hair, well-formed eyebrows over dark brown eyes, small nose, and oval face. As in the Punjab, it is considered appropriate for married women to wear sarees and for single women to wear suits with trousers, baggy at the top and tapered at the ankles. Kamala Vati always wore sarees; Sudarshan alternated between sarees and suits. I wore the same type of suits, except for rare occasions when I wore a saree for special dress-up events.

Sudarshan and I had a number of memorable escapades during our excursions through India. One was the time we got chased by a cow. Don't ever get chased by an angry Brahmin cow, if you can help it! They can be the meanest, nastiest creatures. Sudarshan and I were suddenly chased by one such animal on a main street of New Delhi at dusk, and we never ran so hard in our lives! We had done nothing to provoke this cow. It simply decided to charge at us, and stopped after about five long city blocks.

One harrowing escapade I shall not forget was the time Sudarshan and I were seated in a rickshaw pulled by a water buffalo with long, curved horns. This is the most common mode of transportation in the more backwoods areas. Suddenly, another rickshaw coming toward the left of ours, with me sitting on the edge, accidentally locked its buffalo's horns with ours, with the two creatures thrashing their heads back and forth to get free, within an inch of my left leg. With a very serious expression on her face Sudarshan calmly said to me, "Don't worry; the drivers will get them free." With my heart in my mouth, I thought I was about to be impaled. Then, without the slightest look of concern, the drivers managed to unlock the great beasts' horns and we drove onward. This casual attitude toward dangerous situations floored me the entire time that I was visiting in India. This is the same impression I received from the local street sweepers, both male and female, walking right in the middle of auto and buffalo-drawn rickshaw traffic, sweeping their huge brooms as they went along. I couldn't imagine how none of them got hurt or run over as they went about their work.

Another memorable occasion that Sudarshan and I experienced was our visit to the Sikh's Golden Temple, which houses the holiest books of the Sikh faith, at Amritsar City. The Sikh faith originally came into being to protect India from the Muslim conquerors over five hundred years ago, and many Sikh males are still wearing a sword at their sides as a symbol of their faith. A turban covers their hair (which is groomed but never cut) and a hair net often encloses the beard. Not only was the entire edifice of the Golden Temple painted white, but the tiled floors, pathways, and bridges were spotlessly clean. We were all required to remove our shoes and stockings and bathe our feet before entering the temple grounds, and caretakers did not allow anyone with skin diseases of the feet to enter. We remained barefoot throughout the visit. The holy books of the faith were enshrined in a large room covered with white veil curtains, with three wise elders of the faith there to bestow blessings and answer any questions about the faith. They were seated cross-legged on pillows.

The Sikhs lay claim to their share of geniuses. One of them was Jai Singh II, the king who built the Jaipur City Palace, a tremendous architectural feat. He was also an accomplished soldier, historian, and scientist.

The Sikhs are very conservative people. For example, a married woman is always expected to cover her face when in the presence of her father-in-law or her brothers-in-law, much like the Punjabi Brahmins, whose women must cover their faces in the presence of any male relative from their husband's side of the family. Having a male cousin visiting with us in New Delhi was awkward. The instant he stepped into a room, all the ladies rushed to cover themselves with their sarees.

The next memorable adventure Sudarshan and I shared was our trip to Chandigarh, which is the capital of both Punjab and the adjacent state of Haryana. Here are located the famous Chandigarh rose gardens. However, as we were there in November, all we got to see were twigs. At night, though, the hospitable family of Dr. Uppal, a gynecologist-obstetrician, took us sightseeing, by rickshaw, to the ultra-modern Chandigarh University. The complex of cement buildings housing the colleges of engineering, liberal arts, and medicine were the first and only modern buildings I would get to see during my brief stay. They were attractively lit up at night, and beyond that we got to see a lovely lake with the Himalaya mountains in the distance. We also got to drive through a modern boulevard, with fairly modern book shops, drug stores, and food shops on the sidelines, as well as the fruit and vegetable market.

Dr. Uppal, a lady who has treated many indigent patients gratis, treated Sudarshan and me as if we were her own daughters, though we were only the neighbors of her daughter, who lived upstairs from us in our bungalow in Jullundur. I found a good deal in common intellectually with Saroj, Dr. Uppal's daughter-in-law, who is herself very well educated and spoke English fluently. We got to talking about education in the West, contrasted with education in the East, about our families, about birth control, jewelry, and dress making. During the course of conversation,

Saroj mentioned to me that her father had recently passed away, and for this reason she was wearing only clothes with subdued colors. I said that at least he had lived to see his newly born grandson. Sudarshan immediately corrected me by saying that in India a male child was worthy of being called a grandchild only if he was a son's son. Primogeniture and male dominance still rank very high in Indian culture, notwithstanding the social changes brought about by the Mahatma Gandhi.

Left to right: The author; Sudarshan; Saroj (our hostess) holding her son, and Saroj's mother-in law, Dr. Uppal, on their balcony in Chandigarh, India.

The only things that spoiled part of our trip (and canceled my planned trip to Bombay), were attacks of bacillary and amoebic dysentery, illnesses that run rampant in India, causing severe abdominal cramps and diarrhea, which are quite debilitating. A year later I found out that taking a dose of Sulfonamide medication for ten days before coming to India would have enabled my intestinal flora to withstand the polluted Indian food and water. I lost nine pounds in the process. I also had a bad head cold at the time. Because of this I ended up having to spend a day and night prostrate in a Chandigarh hotel, till I recovered. The Sikh hotel manager was extremely accommodating to me, though I was taken aback by a huge rat that scampered across the table opposite mine in the hotel dining room.

Sudarshan's and my visit in the city of Kartarpur with the Patak family, close friends of Sudarshan's family, was memorable in that I received the kindest ministrations from Mrs. Patak, a widow. Here, unfortunately, I got the worst attack of dysentery, and Mrs. Patak, notwithstanding her impoverished state, hovered over me, feeding me boiled rice and tea, and trying to soothe me. Tarsem Patak told me that were it not for his meager income, his mother and sister would starve. In the dead of the night Sudarshan and the Pataks carted me, folded up in a fetal position in pain, on a bicycle to their doctor, who loaded me with phenobarbital, antispasmodics, and a narcotic, gratis. At that point, I did not care what he gave me, as long as the pain and diarrhea stopped. The doctor said he felt that he, as a colleague, should treat me gratis, for which I humbly thanked him

It was shortly before leaving India, en route to New Delhi to go to Agra, that I was stricken with an awful head cold, with severe nasal congestion and dripping that was uncontrolled. I had brought some American medicines with me, including antihistamine tablets. However, these in no way could stop the constantly runny nose during the entire nine-hour train ride from Jullundur. In most of India, Western commodities such as tissue paper and toilet paper are nonexistent, except in the big cities, where they are sold at a high price. Thus, after having exhausted my small supply of tissue paper, I began to tear into small pieces a brown paper bag that I had with me, to make it last longer.

I was so beside myself, dripping and feeling miserable during the whole train ride, and not quite knowing what to do, that I was greatly relieved once we got to New Delhi. After checking into my hotel (arrangements having been previously made for me), I immediately set about finding a chemist, or drugstore, and after some searching, found one. There, to my great relief, before my very eyes, was a roll of toilet paper, for the large sum of five rupees. (To Indians, that is like five dollars, though on the international exchange there were then seven rupees to the American dollar.)

I carefully carried the precious package, together with some medications I needed for my cold, back to my hotel. There I took hot tea and collapsed onto my bed, to get badly needed rest and recuperate. It took me twenty-four hours to get back to feeling normal enough for the trip to Agra, on a guided tour to see the Taj Mahal. In the meantime, I dared to venture outside my hotel just a bit and found myself being set upon by some Indian women who said, partly in Hindi and partly in English, "Look at it; it has white skin," and began to pinch my arms as if I were a Martian. I pushed them off angrily and returned to the hotel.

Aside from the modern and ancient relics of India that Sudarshan and I saw, there was the other side of India, and that was the side of poverty. Only if one can learn to temporarily accept these conditions in India can one truly enjoy a visit there. One can learn to accept this as a way of life in a land which still exists, to a large extent, in the seventeenth century. Once when I was walking with Sudarshan in Jullundur, some beggars approached me and I gave a little money to them. At once, as if out of nowhere, came several hundred more, and only with great difficulty was Sudarshan able to get them away from us, as they tugged at our garments and shouted imploringly. I learned not to do that again.

There was another heart-rending situation that I got to observe at our bungalow on an almost daily basis. It was the custom to have on the rooftops built-up brick seats with an opening in the middle to use for defecation. At a certain time every morning a woman, haggard and wearing tattered rags, would climb all the stairs with a large, straw whisk broom and a large shovel in hand, to pick up all the defecation and then carry it down with her, to be sold as manure to farmers. The woman was extremely thin, with very wrinkled skin and somewhat stooped shoulders.

I asked Sudarshan if the lady was in her sixties, and why she was doing this work, to which Sudarshan replied that she was in her late twenties, a widow with children to support, and a member of the achut. Sudarshan further told me that if the woman was lucky, she might be able to bring in fifteen or twenty rupees every two weeks. The poor soul had a look of utter resignation, as well as ignorance, on her face. She was one of the most pathetic human beings I have ever seen.

Through Sudarshan, who was my perpetual interpreter, Kamala Vati (Mama-ji, the "ji" indicating special respect), tried to explain to me that this was the siuation these people were born into, as she was born into the Brahmin life, and it was simply to be accepted as a matter of fact. This I could never do, but I learned to accept it as a situation I could not alter. It is this very caste system that probably helped the Indians to tolerate British rule until India finally gained its independence in 1947.

Wherever Sudarshan, Kamala Vati, and I went together, we saw the poor—sometimes lepers with parts of their faces and hands gone—holding out a tin cup for alms. Once we saw a man with a raw stump of an arm, which Sudarshan explained to me as the probable result of a neighbor's chopping off the arm with an axe after a venomous snakebite, in order to save his life. Here in the United States where medical care is so available, it is hard for us to fathom such privation and horror.

However, there was more of this grim privation for me to see yet. Once in Jullundur, near the railway station, and on two other occasions in New Delhi, we saw young boys who appeared to be about ten years old, sitting in a pushcart, with their arms grossly deformed, seemingly twisted out of shape and small for the boys' size, with tin cups in their laps and an older male, perhaps a brother, standing alongside of them begging for alms. When I asked Sudarshan what was the meaning of this, she told me that though some of the boys were born deformed, others probably had had their arms twisted out of shape by their own mothers when they were quite small, so that they could become beggars when they grew older. Thus a poverty-stricken family would have a source of money coming in, as they knew that they would not likely be able to get jobs to support themselves. Sudarshan told me that this dreadful custom was more common in Pakistan than in India. As a single woman then, I felt horror-stricken to think that any mother who had control of her senses could find it in her heart to torture her own or anyone else's child, even if it meant the difference between eating and starvation.

Also pitiful was the frequent presence of men pulling rickshaws without any sandals on their feet.. As I asked Sudarshan what would happen if they got injured by stepping on broken glass or rocks, she replied that they were much more concerned with bringing in the few paltry rupees than they were about potential injuries. After all, they could not afford shoes, and they had families to support. Thus I got an adequate initiation into the state of poverty and suffering in India.

Nevertheless, Sudarshan, Kamala Vati, and I had had a good time together. As we shopped and cooked together, they taught me about Indian culture. I learned all about the rituals in which a Hindu bride is married, the dowry (which is sometimes quite expensive, even to the point of the bride's family having to give the newlyweds an entire set of furniture), the exchange of gifts between the two families, the giving of sweets, and the sequence of marriage ceremonies. It was fascinating, especially when explained with photographs of an Indian wedding, specifically that of Saroj and Kewal Uppal.

First of all, the bride's girlfriends give her a party, during which they offer her food, which she refuses, to express the sadness she feels at having to leave her parents' home and join the household of her husband. Next, the bride's parents go through the gestures of giving her away to the groom's parents, as she will probably become a member of their household and will be expected to care for them for the rest of their lives, especially when they get older. Then the marriage ceremony takes place the following day, with the bridegroom bedecked in a three-quarter-length brocade coat, seated on a white mare, which he rides to the bride's house, where her family await him.

At the ceremony the wedding saree is pulled over the bride's head so as to completely cover her face, and a female relative leads her by the hand to where the groom and Hindu or Sikh priest are standing for the religious part of the ceremony. A banquet and mutual congratulations from both families are then exchanged, with merry making and family embraces. Lastly, after all the festivities, the groom escorts the bride to his house, where the marriage is consummated. A couple of female relatives of the groom will come to his house the following morning to examine the bed sheets for blood, as evidence of the bride's virginity.

Within this context, on a number of visits that Sudarshan and Kamala Vati and I made to local Hindu temples, I was somewhat taken aback by statues carved in graphic, erotic postures. I was told that these were common throughout India, and that they probably came from the tenet of Tantrism, where sexual intercourse is supposed to lead to ultimate reality. This is strictly within the realm of marriage though. In India, sexual mores are very strict. Behavior in public as well as in private is very conservative. Married men and women do not hug and kiss in public.

Preparation for married life is taught at home. In addition to being taught how to cook and sew clothes for the family, all Indian girls are taught how to embroider bedspreads and garments for their future dowries. I also learned to embroider Indian-style from the ladies of my adopted family, and I will always treasure a saree they had hand-embroidered for their American sister and daughter. If someone were to offer me a thousand dollars for it, I would not sell that saree.

The one memorable place in India that I visited alone was the Taj Mahal, the mausoleum built by the emperor Shajahan as a memorial to his late wife, the Empress Mumtaz Mahal, at Agra. It was as breathtakingly beautiful as it was reputed to be. Bordered on one side by the River Jamuna, it is flanked, some distance away, across a man-made lake, by the smaller Black Taj Mahal, which was also erected by the Emperor Shajahan. The architecture of the Taj Mahal is fascinating, especially in that as we entered through the series of archways that approach the main building, and then walked backwards, we got the feeling that the main building was coming toward us. It was an illusion that all the other tourists, Indian and non-Indian alike, experienced with me, as we compared notes. The whole group of us were on a prearranged bus tour from New Delhi which took us to the Taj Mahal, as well as to many other famous Indian edifices, brought us to a modern restaurant for lunch, and then returned at the end of the day to New Delhi. We all made excellent company for each other, with the exception of one young German man who voiced a hatred for Orientals, and whom we all agreed to ostracize.

The domes, alcoves, and minarets of the Taj Mahal, all of white marble, were reflected perfectly in the man-made pool directly in front of the main building. We were there on a day when there was just a slight breeze, with the sun shining. Inside, the mosaics and tiles were perfectly symmetrical. The grave of the Emperor lay to one side under the dome of the Taj. Exquisitely laid-out gardens of trees, shrubs, and flowers, interspersed with pools, surrounded the entrance to the Taj grounds. The Taj had been so designed as to be seen for miles from almost any angle.

These were not the only monumental works constructed by the Emperor Shajahan. He also built the Red Fort in New Delhi for sitting in state. We were lucky to be able to visit this place, also, so named for the red bricks of which it was entirely constructed, and then painted red. In addition, the Emperor Akbar the Great, grandfather of the Emperor Shajahn, had ordered erected a gigantic capital at Fatepur Sikri (which we did not get to visit) and Agra Fort, which we also saw. It was in the Khas Mahal in the Agra Fort that Emperor Shajahan was imprisoned by one of his sons toward the end of his life. We saw the Taj Mahal clearly from there. As our tour guide described the history of each of the edifices we visited, we were all gripped by the thought of the thousands of slaves who lost their lives in the process of building all these massive structures.

When the day came for Kamala Vati and me to part in order for me to return to the United States, we cried a river together. Having no tissues, we resorted to using her saree to wipe away our tears. Through our perpetual interpreter, Sudarshan, Kamala Vati asked me in Hindi, "Will you come back?" I replied, all choked up, "I'll try." My Punjabi Mama-ji put a five-rupee note into my hand for good luck as I boarded the train for New Delhi. I have that note to this day, together with the other gifts Kamala Vati gave me, including an embroidered red wool shawl. The love that we shared was something beyond any measure.

The legacy that my ex-husband and I inherited from India enriched the rest of our lives. It continued to be a part of our lives after we got to Israel, in our food and clothing customs and our association with fellow Jews from India's Bnai Israel community. Even since my return to the United States with my daughter, no meal is complete without some *masala* (curry) seasoning, and some lime or mango pickled in Indian spices. I stitched several Punjabi suits for my daughter, as well as for myself, which we both have made good use of, and I still very much enjoy wearing a saree and a chorli blouse for festive occasions. They are so feminine.

FOURTEEN

THE BETA ISRAEL: HOME, AT LAST

EXCEPT FOR THOSE WHO SUFFERED FROM THE NAZI HOLOCAUST, NO ONE GROUP OF JEWS HAS BEEN SUBJECTED TO WORSE PERSECUTION AND PRIVATION THAN THE BETA ISRAEL, OR JEWS OF ETHIOPIA. These are Jews who have steadfastly kept strict kashruth, as well as the rest of the laws of Moses. Over the past three thousand years, since the time of the last Jewish king, Gideon, the Beta Israel (often referred to by the demeaning term *Falasha,* which means in Amharic "one who is a stranger in his own land") have strictly observed kashruth, *Brit Millah* (circumcision), *Nidah* (ritual separation and purification at the time of menses), *Bar Mitzvah* (confirmation of a Jewish male at the age of thirteen), Passover, and other important Hebrew rituals.

The Passover observances by the Ethiopian Jews are especially meaningful in that, even without soap as we know it, they boil and scour all their clothes and utensils till they are glistening clean. Then, using a few separate utensils that are only for Passover, they prepare the matzoh and sacrificial lamb outside the *tukul,* or family hut, lest any *chometz* (leavening) from inside the hut should contaminate the Passover meal. When we refer to Ethiopian Jewish society, we refer to an enclosure of family huts, each one a tukul, all centered around a larger hut called the *Mezgid,* which is their equivalent of a synagogue. This is where the Sifrei

Torah, if the village possesses any in Hebrew, are enclosed, and where the men go to pray every Friday night and Saturday, or Shabbat, as well as during Hebrew Holy Days. The women who are not in a state of Nidah come here to pray at these times, also, accompanied by the children. Everyone's head is covered in the Mezgid, for respect to G-d, in the presence of His Holiest of Holies, the Ark containing the Torah scrolls. Where there are no Hebrew Torahs, the scrolls are written in Geez, the written language of Ethiopia, and are scrupulously guarded in the inner recesses of the Mezgid. Among the touching slides Dr. Rodney Falk (a Boston physician and Hebrew scholar) shared with us during his lecture in Boston back in 1981 was one showing a large metal Star of David carefully placed over the entrance of the Mezgid.

The Beta Israel's basic bread item is a flat pita-like bread made from a coarse grain called *teff*, which is ground into a meal from which the bread, or *injera*, is baked over a hot, flat stone. A few other vegetables are cultivated there, but the rocky soil of Gondar and Tigre, plus the Coptic Christians and Muslims forbidding Jews to own and work their own land, makes the Ethiopian Jew's basic diet a very poor one. Meat is eaten only on the Hebrew High Holy Days of Rosh HaShanah, the evening meal preceding the fast of Yom HaKippur, and Passover. Dairy and meat utensils, few as they are, are kept strictly separated for kashruth purposes, and there is a six-hour wait between the eating of dairy and meat, for the same reason. On some rare occasions, meat is prepared before the Sabbath—for example, if a Jewish woman has just given birth, to nourish her and help her get her strength back, or to celebrate the Brit Millah, if a boy child has been born into the family (though the meat will be somewhat dried out eight days later, when the celebration is supposed to take place). If the celebration takes place on the Sabbath, the food will be eaten cold, as the Beta Israel will not break the Sabbath laws by igniting fire in any way.

These observant Jews have been slaughtered by the thousands in the past few centuries by warring Coptic Christians and Muslims for practicing their religion. They are also fellow Jews, some of whom are reported to have chosen to starve to death rather than accept non-kosher food, medicine, and clothes from proselytizing Christians. An observant Jew from anywhere in the world can feel perfectly free to eat in a Beta

Israel home, knowing that all the food prepared is strictly kosher. My daughter, Dalya, and I were privileged to eat from the table of Yitzhak Hadena's family at the immigrant absorption center at Mevasserat Zion on the outskirts of Jerusalem, the day before Passover. We had not been in a warmer, more refined Jewish home since we were the guests of Rachel Cohen at Kfar Bnai Ayeesh, and of Rivka Weiss.

Yet these pious, spotlessly clean fellow Jews are the object of abuse perpetrated by our own Ashkenazi Jews, many of whom have themselves fled from persecution but question the Beta Israel's Jewishness. To this my response is in the Psakai Halacha (rabbinical legal decrees) of the late Rabbi David Ben Shlomo Ibn Abi Zimra (commonly called the Radbaz) of the sixteenth century, the late Israeli Chief Rabbi Abraham Isaac Cook, the late Chief Rabbi of Israel, Isaac Herzog, and more recently, former Chief Sephardic Rabbi, Ovadia Yossef. All have attested to the unquestionable Jewishness of the Beta Israel, as descendants of the tribe of Dan of the twelve tribes of Israel, whose lives and liberty we must save from extinction, and bring them all to the Land of Israel.

In this vein, a number of incorrect rumors, as well as articles in the local Jewish newspapers and elsewhere, have been published, stating, among other falsehoods, that according to the Beta Israel custom, in Ethiopia the bride- and groom-to-be sleep together before the marriage ceremony. This is absolutely false, and I have no reason to doubt the Hadena family's and other Jews' integrity when they have told me that this was not so. A British Jewish writer stated that *Falasha* is the correct term to be applied to the Beta Israel. In fact, all of the Ethiopian Jews with whom I have talked have said that it was a term of great derision, usually used by Gentiles to degrade the Beta Israel as Jews.

Furthermore, though most of the written Hebrew prayer scripts in Ethiopia were in Geez, the written language of that area, yet Gemara, among other Hebrew holy studies, was taught devoutly to all Beta Israel boys to whom these books could be made available. It was back in 1980, when I was first introduced to Zacharias Yona, one of the first Beta Israel to be able to come to the United States to speak at Jewish gatherings and tell of the horrible plight of our fellow Jews in Ethiopia, that Dr. Rod Falk showed us color slides of his then-recent visits to Jewish villages in the Gondar and Tigre sections of Ethiopia, where most of the Jews live.

He also played a heart-rending tape recording of the Beta Israel males reciting, in perfect Sephardic Hebrew, the blessings over bread and wine, as well as the Sabbath blessing. Rod also told us that the Torah scrolls that have been donated to Jews in Ethiopia are zealously cared for and constantly taught to young Jewish men by the few Jews who are well versed in Hebrew. I was singularly impressed by the reading of the Torah by our Ethiopian counterparts in Israel. Dr. Falk, himself an Orthodox Jew, had made his trip to evaluate and help upgrade the lives of the Beta Israel, in his capacity as a member of the Falasha Welfare Association of London, though he had since taken up residence in the United States. He stressed to us the great piety, dignity, and poverty of these fellow Jews, emphasizing that poverty and persecution, rather than primitivism, were at the root of most of the Ethiopian Jews' problems.

It is the primitivism of their neighbors that causes discrimination against the Jews in Ethiopia: Many Ethiopian gentiles consider blacksmithing, which many of our people do there, to be consorting with the devil. Also, when the Communist regime of Mengistu Haile-Mariam took over Ethiopia more than thirty years ago, many of the aristocrats whose land was parceled off to the peasants decided to wreak their fury on the innocent Beta Israel community, who had no say whatever in the matter. Hundreds of Jewish women were raped, and equally large numbers of Jewish males were castrated and murdered. Whole villages of Jews were burned to the ground, often with the people still in them. Combining these persecutions with others that have been perpetrated since 1900, the number is approximately twenty thousand Jewish lives being taken that way. This is only a conservative estimate. In short, this has been a repeat of the Nazi Holocaust, only on a smaller scale. Let no one underestimate the suffering of the Jews of Ethiopia, or of their intense Jewishness.

A brighter note on the rescue of the Beta Israel must be noted here. I had been put in touch with Hannah Levine of the Women's Zionist Organization, who was in charge of clothing for the Beta Israel. The clothing ranged from children's sizes to men's and women's sizes 14 to 16, as our people from Ethiopia are almost all built small. With the invaluable cooperation of Rabbi Joshua and Rebbetzen Sharone Zuber, plus Malka Levine Chaiken and her husband Yona (of blessed memory) and several other Jewish women (including Attorney Alanna Cline, who gave generously), we got together bag by bag, and then box by box, about 500 pounds of the finest, most practical new clothing (which we smudged up, washed, dried, and packed in boxes marked "old, used clothing" so that Hannah would not have to pay taxes on the garments when they arrived in Israel.

Week after week we loaded Rabbi Zuber's station wagon with about six cardboard boxes of the clothes (paid for by the Orthodox Jewish community) and mailed them by ship to Israel at a Brookline, Massachusetts, post office. This was done over a period of more than two months. Mrs. Levine wrote me afterward that all the boxes of clothes were received in good order, without paying taxes. Rabbi and Rebbitzer Zuber (and I, to a lesser extent) had done a great Mitzvah Be Shem Mitzvah Torah.

While in office, former Prime Minister Menachem Begin made every effort not only to integrate Sephardi Jews from other countries, but also to salvage the remnants of the Beta Israel. This, notwithstanding the narrow-mindedness of the former Minister of the Interior, Cr. Y. B., and two certain heads of the department of absorption, who totally rejected bringing the Ethiopian Jews to Israel. There is nothing more disgraceful than for Jews who have themselves escaped from persecution to discriminate between one Jew and another. All the Hebrew people from the farthest reaches of the earth are daughters and sons of Israel.

Furthermore, would that many other Jewish immigrants to Israel gave of themselves and acclimated themselves as fully as do the Ethiopian Jews. Where hundreds of Soviet Jews, in addition to native Israelis, have made the decision to come to the United States, everyone rescued by Operation Moses has gone to and stayed in Israel. There the Ethiopians have immediately set about learning about modern electricity, hygiene facilities, and transportation, and have plunged themselves even more deeply into Hebraic studies. They have also accepted any jobs and lodging that were offered them with great fervor. Their rejoicing at being reunited with the rest of Jewry in the Holy Land has been heartwarming. Before leaving office, former Sephardi Chief Rabbi Ovadia Yossef ordained one Beta Israel man as a rabbi, and a number of young Beta Israel men have taken courses at and graduated from the Hebrew University of Jerusalem and Ramat-Aviv University. Of course, all young men from the Ethiopian

Jewish community, as well as all other Israeli men, have done their share of service in the Israeli Defense Forces, and unfortunately a number have paid for it with their lives. This is the substance of which a great and truly Jewish homeland for all Jews of the world is made. Finally, this group of deeply religious, persecuted Jews has been accepted into Israeli society. Until the advent of Operation Solomon, many of them had daily faced the grim reminder that they might never see again their parents and other loved ones who had been killed in Ethiopia or who still languished in poverty and torment in the Gondar, Tigre, and Ambober regions of Ethiopia. Their parents had sent them out of Ethiopia, telling them, "Go to Aretz Kedosha (the Holy Land) to be united with our brethren Jews, though we will never be able to join you." Furthermore, the above-mentioned places are located in extremely rugged, mountainous terrain, accessible only by mules or on foot. Those Jews who were brought to Israel via Operation Moses and then via Operation Solomon did not simply get there by massive plane lifts. Large numbers of them had walked as much as a hundred miles, through the most dangerous terrain, with the blood streaming from their cut and blistered feet, as they traversed burning sands and jagged, rocky areas on their way to reaching Addis Ababa and in some cases, the Sudan. Those less fortunate perished on the way. For such self-sacrificing fellow Jews, we must continue all efforts, financial and spiritual, to help them. This must include enrollment in Sephardi yeshivot and resettlement in kibbutzim and other homes of their own choosing.

One issue remains to be mentioned, that of more than a thousand Ethiopian Jews who are said to have converted to Christianity and are still in Ethiopia. While we do not deny fellow Jews the right to come to Israel, we cannot accept those who have perpetrated blasphemy by conversion, either. This is not to Israel's discredit.

Before my daughter and I left the home of the Hadenas, Zimna Berhane's last request of me was to ask the American Jews to set up a fund at Porat Yossef Yeshiva for Ethiopian Jewish boys' education. That was the most pressing matter about which the Beta Israel families were concerned. They thirst for a good Hebraic education. I gave my word to Zimna that I would do my best to achieve that goal. This would be a great mitzvah for American Jews to do for Ethiopian Jews, giving according to what they can afford. According to Jewish law, the greatest mitzvah that a Jew can do, in addition to the saving of lives and the redemption of captives, is to study the Torah. It is certainly a mitzvah to help the people of other lands. However, our first obligation should be to house, feed, clothe, and educate our own brothers and sisters, who are the Jews of Ethiopia, daughters and sons of Israel. The motto of the Jewish Defense League, "Never Again," must not be forgotten, that we should never allow the perpetration of another Holocaust against the Jews, in this case the Beta Israel. Lastly, I quote from the Sephardic Union of America: "Be proud of your Sephardic heritage; it is eminently Jewish."

FIFTEEN

RETURN TO AMERICA

THE RETURN TO AMERICA SINCE MY DIVORCE FROM MY HUSBAND HAS NOT BEEN EASY, BUT IT HAS BEEN BLESSED WITH PERSONAL JOY AND ENRICHMENT DAILY FROM OUR DAUGHTER, DALYA. At times of greatest darkness she has always brought light and comfort to me, as she did when she wrote to her late father.

A bus accident that resulted in serious injury to my back, with subsequent loss of work and financial hardship, complicated the early part of our return to the United States. However, with the help of Rabbi Joshua and Sharone Zuber, who have become more like a brother and sister to me, we managed to pull through it all. Dalya has been a student at New England Hebrew Academy, while I have worked out of a nursing agency, Staff Builders, for the past several years, plus one year as a Spanish-language medical interpreter.

Return to the United States, and to Boston in particular, has brought back many memories of Israel. For example, shopping from the pushcarts for fruits and vegetables in Boston's Haymarket Square constantly reminds me of the shuk at Mahane Yehuda in Jerusalem. Whenever we have a chance to visit the Arnold Arboretum, with its exquisite flower gardens and trees from all over the world, we think of Yaar Yerushalayim. Though Israel has nothing quite equal to the New England Aquarium in Boston, with its dolphin and sea lion shows, and giant tank with a variety of fish, turtles, sharks, and other creatures, we remember Jerusalem's tiny zoo. We also remember the beautiful zoo at Haifa, with its wild boars, camels, monkeys, and tigers, its bird section and snake house. This, incidentally, makes us think of Boston's Franklin Park Zoo, where everyone used to go not only to see the wild animals, but also to enjoy day-long picnics in the beautiful outdoors. Lexington's Museum of Natural History, with many relics of Native American and European-American history, somewhat equates to Jerusalem's Israel Museum. Of course, there are concert halls in Israel where music lovers can enjoy the Israel Philharmonic Orchestra, as we enjoy Boston's Symphony Hall, which houses the Boston Symphony and the Boston Pops Orchestra.

Though this has nothing to do with Boston, as my daughter and I have traveled through New York City's Boro Park and Crown Heights sections, inhabited mostly by Hassidim, we were strongly reminded of the Mea Shaarim section of Jerusalem, primarily occupied by Eastern European Orthodox Jews. Many of the butcher shops, clothing shops, and shops selling religious items in Crown Heights looked almost exactly like those in Mea Shaarim. The big difference there was in the broad, perpendicular streets of New York, as contrasted with the very narrow, winding cobblestone streets of the Mea Shaarim, which buses often have trouble navigating. Yiddish is spoken freely in these places, and it was heartwarming to me to hear that "Mama Lushon," or mother tongue, as Yiddish is referred to, still thrives. It thrives in a number of Jewish bookstores, where one can still find a large variety of the works of Shalom Aleichem, Peretz, and Singer, in both Yiddish and English. I was exhilarated to discover that I could still read fairly well in classical Yiddish.

As for modern shopping malls, Kikar Dizengoff in Tel Aviv came as close as any to Boston's Downtown Crossing mall and Copley Place, where one can find every kind of store—shoe and clothing shops, jewelry shops, joke shops, and sweets shops, as well as abundant bookstores. Only Tel Aviv outdid Boston in Continental-style pastry shops, where you could buy any variety of the most scrumptious (and fattening) chocolate, mocha, and strawberry cakes and cookies—*verboten* to anyone on a strict diet!

Though our daughter was treated to some of these delicacies, my ex-husband and I made it a point to avoid these high-calorie foods.

Concerning institutions of higher learning, the Hebrew University of Jerusalem comes as close as any, with its schools of liberal arts, medicine, and the humanities, to Boston University. Many worthy Arab students, as well as Jewish students, have completed a formal education at the Hebrew University of Jerusalem, I am proud to say. This is in addition to a large number of foreign students who attend the various colleges at both the Hebrew University and Boston University, a feather in the caps of Americans and Israelis.

When Dalya and I revisited Jerusalem during the Passover of 1986, she got on quite well with her Sephardi and Ashkenazi peers. The only problem was that she was lacking in Yiddish, which I have spoken at home only rarely. The many dear friends we visited in the Mea Shaarim section spoke Yiddish almost exclusively, so I ended up interpreting for Dalya and her new-found friends, who took to each other spontaneously. I have always spoken Hebrew with Dalya at home, so that was not a problem, only the Yiddish. Leaving Israel to return to the United States was one of the most difficult things for me to do, as I left an important part of me there.

Returning to the States, we have readjusted to life here. Dalya has proved to be an apt

Dalya at age 17, with her pet guinea pig, Snowflake.

student academically at the New England Hebrew Academy, as well as talented in cooking and helpful in other household obligations. She is learning about the richness of our Sephardic heritage, as well as of our Jewish heritage in general, from books, embroidery, and cookery, so that she will always be proud of it.

However, the return to America has involved not only readjustment to American life, but continued commitment to Jewish and worldwide causes for peace. Though this has caused me some ostracism, I feel committed to the Peace Now movement. I love people, and I love Israel especially. It is the homeland of my people, as well as of many Palestinian people, all of whom have the right to coexist with dignity and security. They have the right to coexist without outside intervention or threats from religious fanatic groups. Many Arabs and Jews in the United States feel the same as I do, as they participate in the movement, in addition to Israeli Jews and Arabs participating in it.

As for Israel's security, thank G-d, Israel remains strong and is a haven for all Jews, from all over the world. It has been a steadfast ally of the United States against Soviet aggression, and has contributed greatly to technological progress, not only in Israel, but also in sharing with many Third World countries. Support for Israel from the Jews of America must never be allowed to wane. In the words of Brigadier General Yehuda Halevy, "Israel's security is more important than the country's loss of sympathy from people who don't know what it means to have only eleven miles between Tel Aviv and the West Bank. Israel cannot afford to lose even one war."[1]

SIXTEEN

THOSE WHO SACRIFICED

THERE IS ANOTHER SPECIAL PAGE IN THE HISTORY OF ISRAEL, AND THAT IS THE THOUSANDS OF JEWS AND OTHERS WHO GAVE OF THEMSELVES SO THAT JEWISH PEOPLE SHOULD LIVE, BUT WHO THEMSELVES NEVER LIVED TO GET TO ISRAEL. It was not only the thousands of Jews who emigrated to Israel from all over the world, but those who came from the Nazi death camps, who made Israel into a nation. There were also many unsung heroes and heroines who braved the worst of elements and physical dangers to save Jewish lives and help create the Jewish state.

The story of one such martyr, Dr. Henryk Goldschmidt, more commonly known by his Polish pseudonym, Janus Korczak, is movingly told by Betty Jean Lifton in a *New York Times Magazine* article, "Shepherd of the Ghetto" (April 20, 1980). Dr. Goldschmidt remained steadfast in his devotion to his two hundred Jewish war orphans, whose home he founded, together with his friend, Stepha Wilczynska. He, Stepha, the eight teachers of the orphanage, and the children were herded by German and Ukrainian guards from the Warsaw Ghetto onto the train that would take them and four thousand other Jewish children to Treblinka, to be gassed to death. That was on August 6, 1940. It was rumored that a member of the Gestapo, recognizing Dr. Goldschmidt as the author of the book *Child of the Salon,* an exposé of the horrid conditions of the children in the Warsaw slums, offered him his freedom, but that he refused, insisting on remaining with his orphans unto death. At one point in the Warsaw Ghetto, when Dr. Goldschmidt was actually offered his freedom, he replied, "You do not leave a sick child in the night, and you do not leave children at a time like this." For this reason, Dr. Goldschmidt has come to be considered by the people of Israel as one of the Thirty-Six Just Men who, according to Jewish tradition, bring about the world's salvation by their nobility of spirit.

Dr. Goldschmidt had put himself through medical school, during which time he got to observe and write about the horrors of the Warsaw slums. As a result of this exposure, he founded Polish orphanages and the first national children's newspaper, lectured at the University of Warsaw on childcare, and spoke in court on behalf of children's rights. Only his *Ghetto Diary*, translated into English, now remains.

Ms. Lifton's article records yet another moving anecdote. Dr. Goldschmidt showed an orphan, under fluouroscopy, to university students, with the child's heart beating rapidly. He said to them, "Don't forget this sight. Before you raise your hand to a child, before you administer any kind of punishment, remember what his frightened heart looks like." In Treblinka, where over a million Jewish men, women, and children were put to death, only one person's name is inscribed on a stone; it reads, "Janus Korczak (Henryk Goldschmidt) and the Children."

There is another hero in Jewish history, a Swedish Christian named Raoul Wallenberg, who saved over a hundred thousand Hungarian Jews during the Nazi Anschluss. In July 1944, Raoul left Sweden to serve as a diplomat in Hungary, working under Carl Ivar Danielsson, head of the Swedish embassy there, to set up rescues of Jews by means of Swedish passes, which provided protection to prevent deportation to the Nazi death camps, and also to allow emigration to neutral countries. Before Raoul left Sweden, chief Rabbi Marcus Ehrenpreis gave him the Talmudic blessing: "Those who are on a mission for good deeds are protected from harm. May G-d bless thee and preserve thee. . . May the Lord lift up His face unto thee and give thee peace."[1] Shortly afterward, Raoul used his diplomatic skills to persuade Hungarian Regent Horthy to order deportations stopped on July 7, 1944, as well as to honor five thousand Swedish safety passports.

There was an area of Budapest where Raoul acquired a number of "safe" houses, the most outstanding being one at 6 Tatra Street, where relief work for the refugees, including medical care, social service, board, housing, and hospitalization in cooperation with the Red Cross were provided. Here at one point thirty-three thousand Jews were cared for, between the Swedes, the Swiss, and the Red Cross. Here much credit is due the late Swiss Consul, Charles Lutz, also, who issued eight thousand Swiss passes. Lutz, Moshe Krausz, and Arthur Weiss set up a rescue in a mirror company called the "Glass House," through which two thousand lives were saved.[2]

This system worked till the Nyilas, or Arrow Cross government (so called because of the arrows affixed at each end of the Cross, their symbol) took over from Horthy. New Hungarian leader Szalasi instituted a reign of terror with mass deportations. Young thugs of the Arrow Cross were not stopped from beating Jews to death with rifle butts and stuffing Jews into barrels of cold water and freezing them to death. Even then, Raoul followed death marchers with trucks of food, clothing, and medicine, and pulled out people he could declare Swedish, acts which antagonized Adolph Eichmann, the Nazi then in charge of the "final solution" in Hungary, to no end. Throughout all these endeavors, Per Anger and Lars Berg remained Raoul's two most steadfast companions.[3]

Shortly thereafter, the Russians invaded Hungary and put an end to Arrow Cross rule. However, when Raoul attempted contact with them, he and Per Anger were arrested, on the grounds of being German spies, presumably. Knowledgeable sources believed that it was because of Raoul's having received funds from the War Refugee Board in Washington. This was at the onset of the Cold War, with Russia's anti-American feelings running very high. It is now almost sixty years since Raoul's imprisonment in the Soviet Gulag, with many conflicting reports of his status. Per Anger, who has long since been freed, former Swedish Prime Minister Taj Erlander, and current Israelis, who had been in cell blocks near Raoul's, believe he died about ten years ago. Raoul's half-brother, Dr. Guy Von Dardel, and half-sister, Nina Lagergren, fought steadfastly till the end for his release.[4]

One thing that human rights activists have known was that the Soviet Union did respond to public pressure. Were all the Jews in the world, especially those of the United States, working in conjunction with their Congressmen and Senators, to have started a concentrated campaign to free Raoul, it probably would have worked. So often have we Jews complained of the insensitivity of the goyim. Now when finally a gentile appeared who sacrificed his life to save Jews, we have answered his suffering with apathy. For this there can be no forgiveness. Lastly, in regard to Raoul Wallenberg, we must remember the Talmudic dictate, "The righteous of all creeds and beliefs in the world are looked upon as just people by G-d."

Another such martyr, Major General Lev Dorator of the Russian army, brings back memories of many true stories told to my cousins and me by Mama Tzipah. She recalled that, as a young girl in Russia, she knew of many Jewish boys who were kidnapped by the Russians at age three, to be conscripted into the Russian army, and never again seen by their parents. The treatment of these boys was said to have been so brutal that some young Jews would willingly allow friends to remove one of their eyes (with or without anesthesia) to avoid conscription. However, there were some young Russian Jews who braved the elements, and were conscripted into the Russian army. Lev Dorator was one of them. He served as Major General of the head Cossack division at Rostov, defeating the Nazis there, and being killed in the process. This battle smashed the strength of the Nazis on the Eastern front, and for this valor General Dorator was posthumously awarded Russia's highest military honor. In spite of Russia's anti-Semitism, there were a number of Jews who led in their armed forces. These included Yacub Smushkevich, former chief of the Soviet Air Force, and Gregory Stern, former Chief of the Army in the Far East, to mention only a few.[5]

People who are familiar with recent Jewish history recall the name of Hannah Senesch, the Hungarian Jewess who, together with Eliahu Golomb, Enzo Sereni, and others, numbering thirty in all (in what was then Palestine), volunteered for a parachute corps, under the British. They were dropped into Europe to rescue Allied troops who had been shot down, as well as Jews who were in hiding. Ultimately, only seven of that rescue group were to survive. These people were chosen to attempt rescues in Hungary, Slovakia, Romania, and Bulgaria, because they came from the Balkans, whose lands and languages they knew well. There were over a million Jews in these areas.

Hannah and two men of the parachute corps made their way through two hundred miles of enemy territory, until a spy posing as a partisan guide betrayed Hannah. She was then sent to a Budapest prison, where she gave out no information, even under torture. Refusing a blindfold, Hannah was shot to death at the age of twenty-three. Her poem has come to be the favorite poem of Israel. It reads:

Blessed is the match consumed in lighting the flame,
Blessed is the flame that burns in the secret fastness of the heart,
Blessed is the heart with strength to stop beating for honor's sake,
Blessed is the match consumed in lighting the flame.[6]

Enzo Sereni was accidentally dropped into German territory (instead of North Italy), was captured and sent to Dachau, where he and other Italian prisoners were shot. His wife, Ada, also an Italian Jewess, was instrumental in saving many hundreds of Jewish lives via illegal immigration, through her connections with certain people in the Italian government. All in all, though the majority of the parachute corps met with a bitter end, they had succeeded in rescuing and directing for ship travel thousands of European Jews and Allied troops, before they were captured and, in some cases, tortured to death.[7]

One last person to mention among the unsung heroines of the time of the Holocaust was Ruth Aliav, a member of the Mossad. This was the Palestinian-based Jewish group that was responsible for rescuing and transporting Jewish refugees by sea. This was often done by means of ships that were barely seaworthy, under the most dangerous circumstances, and often with inadequate sanitation, food, clothing, and medical equipment. This special breed of daredevils, including Ruth Aliav, Moshe Agami, and Munya Mardor, to name only a few, had to use every bit of initiative, courage, and ability to improvise. They had to outwit the Nazis and the British ships sent specifically to turn back Jewish ships from Palestine. Often there were more failures than successes. One of the most brutally glaring of those failures, in December of 1941, was the sinking of the Struma, a cattle boat with seven hundred sixty-nine Jewish men, women, and children aboard, off Istanbul, Turkey. Only one person survived the sinking, and neither the Turks nor the British made any effort to rescue at least the seventy children on board, before the Turkish police seized the ship and the boilers exploded.

On a more positive note, Ruth Aliav succeeded in persuading King Carol II of Romania to release the *Tiger Hill,* a vessel filled with fourteen hundred Polish Jewish refugees, to sail to Palestine from Romanian waters. However, the British fired on the *Tiger Hill* when it reached Tel Aviv, and three people were killed. Ruth Aliav and others of the Mossad did live to reach the Promised Land.

All these people who gave their lives as parachutists, or fighting on foreign fronts, or operating out of the Mossad have been the real heroes and heroines of Israel. Fellow Jews like my colleagues and me, who came in the 1960's and 1970's, had never before known the meaning of real suffering and deprivation, having come from the relative comfort and security of the United States, Venezuela, France, and Argentina.

EPILOGUE

As I review the struggles and abuses I suffered as a child and the mistakes I made later as a result of them, I look back at the anger that turned into caring for others less fortunate than I. That anger gnawed away at me until, with the understanding and compassion I received from Dr. Thomas Morris, Jr. (of blessed memory), I was able to redirect that anger into caring for the sick and wounded during the Yom Kippur War. Finally, my resentment of my parents was turned into true love between my husband, Simon, and me. Had it not been for my mother-in-law's coming between us, that love might have lasted.

As for my moral convictions, I have come to base them on the examples set by some of the people I have met, as well as the suffering humanity that I have learned about from them and that I myself have observed. I believe there is room enough for everyone to coexist peacefully on earth, though many nations continue to try to subdue others, as the former Soviet Union did to Afghanistan, as the Ethiopian Marxist government has done to Eritrea, and as the People's Republic of China has done to Tibet. The State of Israel has sought no territorial gain; it has sought only to be let alone within the security of its own borders.

The citizens of the Russian-led Confederacy of Republics have been exposed to far more of the horrors of war than have the people of the United States. I have learned from my neighbor, Dr. Victoria Vasilkovskaya, about the unspeakable horrors that her family were exposed to in 1942, during the Second World War. The Nazis had blockaded Leningrad then, allowing no food or other lifesaving supplies to get through, and Victoria's grandmother was among the fortunate few who were helped to escape. Others were less fortunate, though. During the severe winter of that year, a hundred thousand people of Leningrad would starve to death. People were reduced to such subhuman levels that the most unspeakable savagery took place. Some turned to cannibalism, which Victoria's grandmother witnessed. After someone had fallen dead on the streets, another person would cut up the body for meat, and then rush away with it to consume it clandestinely. This was not common practice, but it did occur during these most horrendous of circumstances. Also, we must not forget that the Russians lost over twenty million men, women, and children from the German onslaught in the Second World War, known to the Russians as the "War of the Fatherland." This was how Josef Stalin, hated though he was for cruelty to his own people, came to be praised for keeping his word to free Leningrad, which he did by leading the Russian battalions to break through the Nazi-held lines surrounding the city.

Americans have become sensitive about being attacked only since Osama bin Ladin's destruction of the World Trade Center on September 11, 2001. They understand in a new way the experience of other nations who have been attacked, particularly those who suffered from World War II on their own soil, whether in Europe, Asia, Africa, or elsewhere. Perhaps we all need a reminder of what war is really like, and what profits it does not reap, except for the industrialists. Unlike movie scenes of war, there is no glory or glamour, in either hand-to-hand or more distantly directed combat. Whether we use broadswords, fixed bayonets, or remotely controlled drones, we cease to be human beings when we reduce others, or are ourselves reduced, to pieces of flesh as bodies are impaled or chunks of flesh are torn from them, or they are consumed in flames.

Here are some of my thoughts, combined with the insights of some who lived to return from battle and shared their experiences with me. At the end of the battle there is utter silence, save for the groans of the wounded and the dying. Many severely wounded men and women lie crying in agony, with no one to give them any medical attention or ease their pain. There is death and desolation all around you. The stench of the dead bodies, which combines body odor with the smell of feces and vomitus, permeates the air to the point where there is no escaping from it, and it chokes the strongest person. The bodies of the dead turn into a festering mass, to become food for vultures.

The dreams of thousands of young people have been blown apart forever. For them there is no return. There are no names, no titles, no status symbols any more. There is no one to whom you can call out. Numerous innocent civilians have been killed. You want to go home, but there is no home to which you can return. Everything has turned to darkness, strangeness, and gripping isolation. There's nothing familiar anymore, no person or place that we recognize. We walk and walk endlessly through the darkness, past the charred, mangled bodies of men, women, and children, past rubble that was once buildings, homes, and schools, through irreversible, grim silence and desolation. You become numb to your own hunger and dirt, your own physical and mental exhaustion. Only the pain continues, and the thirst tearing at your parched throat till that's all you can think of, except desolation.

The recollections of many people I have known who served in the Korean and Vietnam wars are incredibly similar to my own recollections of war. Only those who returned from the Vietnam War said that the abominations they were subjected to or observed were absolutely horrific, beyond what other war veterans had recalled. This is what we all have to look forward to—in the words of the late President John F. Kennedy, "a war where the survivors would envy the dead"—unless the nations of the world agree on nuclear disarmament and disarmament of germ and chemical warfare. The Middle East has been a political hot spot for many years, and the instability of the region has increased recently because of the nuclear arms threat and the violent anti-Semitism of Iran's President Mahmoud Ahmadinejad, as well as the U.S. war in Iraq.

There are no easy answers to these dilemmas. Forty-five years ago, a wise history professor of mine at Boston State College, Dr. Paul Gottlieb, said, "No war is inevitable." I can see his point, in that no nation should initiate aggression unless its existence is being threatened. For one thing, no nation has a right, as a superpower or otherwise, to impose its political will on other nations (such as Tibet) whose religious institutions have kept them intact for centuries. Likewise, modernization does not necessarily have to mean Westernization. The world needs both Western and Eastern institutions and cultures to make it viable.

All the world needs to be grateful to the givers of this world, to the late Dr. and Mrs. Thomas Morris, Jr. for their care of foster children; to Serge and Beate Klarsfeld (French Nazi-hunters who brought Klaus Barbie, the "Butcher of Lyons," who caused thousands of French people to be killed and tortured, to justice); to Mordecai Bar-On and Mohammed Milhelm, who initiated the Peace Now movement; and to Judge Joseph Tauro, savior of the mentally retarded. We need to be grateful also to Mother Teresa, devoted to the care of the "poorest of the poor" in India and elsewhere; and to the inconspicuous social worker, Virginia Rice, who has done so much for bruised and battered and terminally ill children.

Aside from these great givers to humanity, there is an element of completely overlooked, patient sufferers who have paved the way for everyone in civil rights and the rights of mankind, in general. This was very eloquently stated by Marsha Mickens, president of the Bakers and Confectionary Union of the AFL-CIO, as she delivered the keynote address at the tribute to Rev. Dr. Martin Luther King, Jr., on January 16, 1989, at Faneuil Hall in Boston. Ms. Mickens described her trip to Alabama in the oppressive heat and humidity of summer, and her encounter with several elderly African-American ladies, obviously poor, sitting on the steps of a building in Birmingham, the state capital. They were sharing their memories of the first African-Americans who dared to vote and were lynched for it, the feel of the bull whips on their backs, the poverty, the deprivation, the constant fear under which they had to live—and the pathway that they had paved for the rest of us to follow." For in Ms. Mickens's words, "It is to these humble old ladies that we all owe what we have, these old ladies who sat fanning, fanning, fanning, remembering all the agonies they had to live through to make a better life for the rest of us. There, but for the grace of G-d, go you and I, and let none of us ever forget that."

These were some of the most profound words I have ever heard, especially so because they were spoken on the occasion of honoring Dr. King's memory and remembering what he lived and died for, in the name of humanity. It is a pity, in my opinion, that little old ladies of true greatness, such as these spoken of by Marsha Mickens, do not get into our newspapers. I'm glad I brought my daughter with me to this event, so that she may know what America and the civil rights movement are all about and honor one of the greatest Americans, the Reverend Dr. King.

Many newspapers profit by sensationalizing the crimes of the local community and the world. Unfortunately, they do not give enough credit to the humanitarians who give constantly for the betterment of mankind.

Much credit is due to Americans who have helped the underprivileged, such as Dr. Lorraine Hale, who with her elderly mother founded Hale House in New York, to care for crack babies (born to mothers whose addiction to crack was passed on to the children) out of her own pockets. Also, Harold Cornwall, who has devoted much of his life to the Wilderness Scouts, a group of local teenagers from the backwoods of Appalachia, should be remembered for founding this group. He not only takes the young men on outings, but also has them help the elderly in their own communities, by chopping wood for them and helping them in other ways. Lastly, Henry Vargas should be remembered and honored for founding the Camp Kilpatrick Mustangs, a football team of boys who were juvenile thugs, and transforming them into productive young citizens with respect for their community in Los Angeles. All of these unsung heroes and heroines deserve much praise and appreciation from all of us, for it is they who make the world a fit place to live in for all. They have confronted injustices and made life worth living for millions of oppressed people.

It is they who must inherit the earth, for they have risked their own lives, without thought of compensation, in order that others may have a better life. And such people of love and peace are to be found in Boston and Jerusalem, and in many other places throughout the world where good people of all races and creeds exist.

NOTES

Chapter Three

1. Father Thomas J. Carroll, *Blindness* (Boston: Little, Brown, 1961).

Chapter Five

1. Margaret Truman Daniels, *Women of Courage* (New York: William Morrow, 1976), 59-72.
2. John Bakeless, *The Adventures of Lewis and Clark* (Boston: Houghton Mifflin, 1962), 190.
3. Judith Gaines, "Warrior in the Modern World," *Boston Globe Magazine,* August 28, 1988.
4. Dee Brown, *Bury My Heart at Wounded Knee* (New York: Holt, Rinehart, and Winston, 1970), 443-45.

Chapter Seven

1. Anwar El-Sadat, *In Search of Identity* (New York: Harper & Row, 1977), 3.

Chapter Eight

1. Anwar El-Sadat, *In Search of Identity* (New York: Harper & Row, 1977), 312.
2. Ibid., 82.
3. Martin Gallanter, "View From a Different Angle," *Boston Jewish Times,* April 7, 1988.

4. David Landau and Gil Sedan, *Jewish Advocate* (Boston), June 2, 1988.
5. Mary Curtius, "General Mitzna," *Boston Sunday Globe,* March 20, 1988.
6. Arthur Jahnke, "Israel's Black Americans: Cult or Culture?" *The Real Paper* (Boston), May 5, 1979.
7. Albert Vorspan, *Giants of Justice* (New York: Union of American Hebrew Congregations, 1960), 137.
8. Ibid.
9. *Jewish Advocate,* November 19, 1981, 1, 23.

Chapter Eleven

1. Robert Goldston, *Next Year in Jerusalem* (Boston: Little, Brown, 1978), 29.
2. Ibid., 30, 31.
3. Ibid., 31.

Chapter Twelve

1. Franklin H. Littell, *Wild Tongues* (Toronto: MacMillan, 1969), 8.
2. Ibid, 9.
3. Edwin Black, "The Legacy of Hatred: Martin Luther and the Jews," *Jewish Advocate,* October 16, 1986.
4. Ibid.
5. Hillel Levine and Lawrence Harmon, *The Death of an American Jewish Community* (New York: Free Press, 1992), 263.
6. Ibid, 267.

Chapter Fifteen

1. Jane Weingarten, *Jewish Advocate,* June 2, 1988, 4.

Chapter Sixteen

1. Harvey Rosenfeld, *Raoul Wallenberg, Angel of Rescue* (Buffalo: Prometheus Books, 1982), 28.
2. Ibid., 37, 38.

3. Ibid., 110-12.
4. Ibid., 140-44.
5. *Jewish Family Almanac* (New York: F. F. F. Publishers, 1942), 157-58.
6. Hannah Senesh, *Hannah Senesh, Her Life and Diary* (New York: Schocken Books,1966), 256.
7. Ibid., 197.

About the Author

Saralea Zohar grew up in Chelsea, Massachusetts, and graduated with distinction from the Whidden School of Nursing in 1965. During her first trip to Israel (1968-69) she obtained international reciprocity as a State Registered Nurse. In 1971 Saralea traveled in India. At the outbreak of the Yom Kippur War in 1973 she returned to Israel and served as a triage nurse in some of the war's bloodiest battles.

Saralea married Simon Aaron in Jerusalem in 1974, and in 1975 gave birth to their daughter, Ruth. She returned to Massachusetts in 1976 and has since been active in aiding Native Americans and Ethiopian Jewry.

www.ingramcontent.com/pod-product-compliance
Lightning Source LLC
Chambersburg PA
CBHW072134270326
41931CB00010B/1762